The Duffer's Guide to t

Josephine Laffin graduated from the University of Adelaide in 1990 with an MA in history. She is currently Church History lecturer for the Flinders University of South Australia and the Adelaide College of Divinity.

Praise for Josephine Laffin's
The Duffer's Guide to the Old Testament

'Is the Old Testament dull and irrelevant? Certainly not here – a marvellous guide to the Old Testament and modern approaches to it, for duffers at all levels! It's both funny and serious – Josephine Laffin has a marvellous gift for bringing modern study of the Bible to life, and a unique gift of making you laugh and think.'

DR PHILIP JOHNSTON, *Wycliffe Hall, Oxford*

'Josephine Laffin shows good insight into questions real students ask and provides a very user-friendly way of exploring the issues raised.'

MARY J. EVANS, *London Bible College*

' ... raises important questions about Old Testament interpretation in a provocative and arresting way.'

REV DR MIKE BUTTERWORTH, *Oak Hill College*

The Duffer's Guide to the Old Testament

Josephine Laffin

Marshall Pickering
An Imprint of HarperCollins*Publishers*

Marshall Pickering is an Imprint of
HarperCollins*Religious*
Part of HarperCollins*Publishers*
77–85 Fulham Palace Road, London W6 8JB

First published in Great Britain
in 1996 by Marshall Pickering

1 3 5 7 9 10 8 6 4 2

A catalogue record for this book is
available from the British Library

ISBN 0 551 02947 1

Printed and bound in Great Britain by
Caledonian International Book Manufacturing Ltd, Glasgow

Scripture quotations are taken from the New Revised Standard Version,
Copyright © 1989 by the Division of Christian Education of the National Council
of the Churches of Christ in the United States of America.

Contents

Acknowledgements

First, my grateful thanks to Christine Smith, Editorial Director at Marshall Pickering, for asking me to write this book. Throughout the writing process I have been torn between excitement at being given the opportunity to do it, and awe at the magnitude of the task. The Bible is a rather exceptional book! Years of scholarship would be required to do justice to it. I am afraid that I have not had that time, and I do not regard myself as a biblical scholar. If anything, I am a historian, but along with teaching church history I have had the opportunity in the last few years to study for a Bachelor of Theology degree. I would like to express my very great appreciation to Professor Norman Habel and the Revd Dr John Roffey for their fascinating and inspiring lectures on the Old Testament. Thank you, too, to Marie Turner, Steven Ogden, and Anne Roder, tutors for Old Testament subjects, and to all the students who have studied with me. Some of you may discover comments on the following pages which seem vaguely familiar. I once read somewhere (I'm afraid I can't remember where) that writers are thieves – they steal conversations. I am certainly guilty of that! However, the characters in this book are all fictional and not meant to represent real people.

Finally, I would like to thank Frank Anderson for

permission to use lines from the song 'Strong and Constant' (from the collection *Eagles Wings* (1989), published by Chevalier Music, 51 Mailey St, West Sunshine, Australia 3020). The extract from Ernesto Cardenal's poem 'Why Have You Left Me?' (from *Poems* (1981), translated by John Griffiths, published by the Crossroad Publishing Company, New York) is reprinted by permission of Search Press Limited.

WEEK·ONE

The Word of God?

I came home from my first Old Testament tutorial with my head reeling. The Bible sure is a complex book. There are so many different opinions that I am totally confused. Perhaps if I go over the discussion again it will help.

Liz, our tutor, welcomed us to the course. She admitted that this is her first time as a tutor. She's still studying herself and she stressed that she wasn't an 'expert' and she didn't intend to do all the talking. The purpose of the tutorials is to give us the opportunity to discuss our reading and reflection, and to learn from each other. To 'facilitate the sharing process', Liz suggested that we start with a 'getting to know you' session. Could we each say something about ourselves?

Frank, with a pleased expression, said that it was seven years since he was saved.

'From what? Drowning?' asked Jason flippantly.

'Eternal damnation,' said Frank in a tone of stern reproof.

Christobel, with an airy wave, said that she didn't believe in all that fire and brimstone stuff. Wade agreed, Melinda looked disapproving, and Maureen said rather viciously that she hoped that there was a hell for husbands who left their wives for younger women. Melinda then thanked God that her husband would never commit adultery because he is a Christian, whereupon Maureen advised her that she wouldn't trust a man as far as she could throw him, Christian or otherwise. This prompted Ruth to say that perhaps it was just as well that she doesn't have a husband. She is a nun.

Dave revealed that he doesn't have a husband either, but he has got a dog – a German Shepherd called Otto. He supposed that Otto ought to be Lutheran, given his Scandinavian-style name, but so far his only interest in religious matters seems to be chasing Jehovah's Witnesses down the street.

Not to be outdone, Jason disclosed that he has a six-foot long carpet python called Deidre. They are both agnostics, but prepared to listen to a wide variety of religious views. Strangely enough, two Mormons, when given the opportunity to hold Deidre while expounding their beliefs, had turned and fled.

Kirsty, staring at Jason with a mixture of horror and fascination, confided that she has a budgie called Tweetie Pie. She's trying to teach him to speak. She hasn't had much luck yet, although he does seem to like listening to her Amy Grant tape. I said that I have a cat called Tiger. His only interest in life appears to be food.

After some speculation about what would happen if Otto, Deidre, Tweetie Pie and Tiger ever became acquainted with one another, Liz managed to ask another question: 'When you first hear the word "Bible" what do you immediately think?'

'The Word of God!' proclaimed Frank. 'God said it. I believe it. That settles it!'

'I am simply filled with awe and gratitude when I think how God has graciously provided us with knowledge of himself,' declared Melinda. She held up her copy of the Bible. 'This wonderful book is the inspired, inerrant, authoritative, clear, self-interpreting, self-authenticating, and sufficient for all time communication of God to man.'

'And men can have it,' muttered Christobel.

Liz began to get that rather strained look that Derek, our church history tutor, often has.

'What exactly do people mean when they say that the Bible is inspired?' demanded Maureen. 'Did God sit up in heaven dictating to his secretaries on earth, like my ex-husband used to do? And that's not all he used to do with them, either,' she added darkly.

'Maureen, when we talk about the Bible being "inspired" we mean that the Holy Spirit guided both the biblical writers' thoughts and the words they used,' answered Melinda. 'However, God graciously took into account the writers' different backgrounds and styles. The miracle of Scripture is that God could communicate his infallible revelation through fallible men without violating their individual personalities. I never cease to wonder at it. Thus, in the 66 books of the Bible, God used many different writers (some living hundreds of years apart), different languages (Hebrew, Aramaic, and Greek), and different types of writing (law, history, prophecy, poetry, biography, and so on), but, overall, there is an amazing harmony and unity that could only be achieved if there was ultimately the one divine author.'

'Harmony! Unity!' exclaimed Wade incredulously. 'The Bible is riddled with inconsistencies, contradictions, and errors. Biblical scholars in the last hundred years or so have shown what manifestly *human* works the biblical writings are.'

'On the contrary,' maintained Melinda with an air of calm certainty, 'provided that scholars do not approach the Bible with an anti-christian bias, the difficulties that they find are very few in number. They have doubtless arisen due to minor problems with language and translation.'

'Salvation is hardly a minor theme in the Bible,' said Wade, sitting back with his arms crossed. 'So are we saved by faith alone, as Paul wrote, or by works as Matthew 25 and James 2 indicate? Luther at least recognized the contradiction, and would have liked to have chopped James out of the New Testament!'

'Luther had a fetish about certain texts,' responded Melinda, her calm unimpaired. 'Unfortunately, heresies have arisen because people have focused on single texts and not taken into account the whole body of inspired teaching. I am not saying that Luther was a heretic, but we must understand that the Bible is a harmonious whole that reveals God's revelation progressively throughout. One scriptural passage explains another. Thus, we are saved by faith alone, but true Christian faith naturally leads us to do good works.'

'Guided by the Holy Spirit,' affirmed Frank.

'Well, you cannot deny that the Bible is often interpreted differently by different people,' contended Wade with a sarcastic laugh. 'The claim in the Protestant Reformation that Scripture was clear and self-interpreting was a joke. Even the main reformers bitterly disagreed on certain points!'

'While there are some difficulties in Scripture, the passages which relate to salvation are quite clear,' retorted Melinda.

'Yes. Clearly different,' said Wade.

'Ah, but we mustn't forget that Satan is always trying to deceive us,' warned Frank. 'Remember how he twisted Scripture to try to trap Jesus after his baptism.'

Melinda nodded.

'But all the miracles and fulfilled prophecies throughout the Bible prove that it is the Word of God,' went on Frank exuberantly. 'One of the miracles was the sun standing still for a day so that Israel could be victorious over its enemies (Judges 10). My pastor was only saying the other day that some American scientists were calculating the positions of the sun, moon, and stars over the centuries with the help of a computer, and the computer discovered that 23 hours and 20 minutes was missing from history which couldn't be accounted for. Then one of the scientists (who was a Christian) thought of Judges 10, but the missing time was still 40 minutes short of a day. Then he remembered that when Hezekiah asked for a sign that God would heal him he was given a choice of the sun going backward or forward 10 degrees. 10 degrees is exactly 40 minutes! So that explains the missing day! Don't you think that's fantastic?'

Frank looked around expectantly.

'It certainly is,' said Jason scornfully. 'Since when has the sun moved? And how do you know that the computer wasn't programmed to miss a day? That stupid hoax has been around for years. It's only spread by dodgy evangelists.'

Frank glared at him.

'Of course, Christians do not need to go in search of proofs for the inspiration of Scripture,' intervened Melinda. 'God confirms this in our hearts through the inward witness of the Holy Spirit.'

Jason looked as though he found this pious response thoroughly revolting, and Christobel appeared almost ready to explode.

'Well, common sense tells me that everything in the Bible can't be direct from God,' said Maureen cheerfully, apparently impervious to the mounting tension. 'I mean, the Ten Commandments and the Sermon on the Mount and all that might be, I suppose, but surely God had better things to do with his time than draw up boring lists of who begat who, what the measurements of the temple should be, what you should do if your donkey falls down a well, and all that sort of thing.'

'But, Maureen, we cannot accept some parts of Holy Scripture as God's Word and reject others,' asserted Melinda.

'Why not?' demanded Wade.

'Because either the Bible is or it is not the Word of God,' Melinda replied. 'If it is, the human mind is hardly competent to make distinctions within it, to presume to judge which sections are God's truth. How dare we challenge the authority of Scripture?'

'*Authority of Scripture!*' burst out Christobel, able to stay silent no longer. 'Yes, we must never forget the authority of Scripture! Appeals to it have justified the persecution of the Jews, the crusades, the inquisition, the torture of heretics, the burning of witches, slavery, and (its most enduring influence) the subordination of women in the home, society, and the Church. This is because the Bible is not the words of God but the words of men, MEN, MEN!'

The last 'men' almost deafened us.

'I could give countless examples of the inferiority and abuse of women in the biblical texts,' Christobel continued passionately, 'but I will just tell one story to illustrate my point.'

She snatched Melinda's Bible from her lap and flicked through it.

'Here we are: Judges 19. A Levite and his concubine are on a journey to his home and they stop for the night at a place called Gibeah. Some men of the city surround the house where they are staying and call out to the owner: "Bring out the man who came to your house so that we can have sex with him." The host replies: "No, my friends, don't be so vile. Since this man is my guest, don't do this disgraceful thing. Look, here is my virgin daughter, and his concubine. I will bring them out to you now, and you can use them and do to them whatever you wish. But to this man, don't do such a disgraceful thing." So the Levite throws out his concubine and they rape and abuse her throughout the night. Eventually they let her go and she staggers back to the house and collapses by the door. Does the Levite rush out to tend to her wounds? No, he does not. He leaves her there until morning, then when he is ready to leave he tosses her poor, battered little body onto the back of a donkey and she has to endure the long journey to his home. Then, he gets a knife and *cuts her into twelve pieces*, so that he can send the pieces to the twelve tribes of Israel to summon them to avenge the insult done to *him*!!! The Israelites rally to his cause, and, fortified with assurances of victory from "the Lord", they embark on an orgy of slaughter, destruction, and rape.'

Christobel dashed a tear from her eye.

'How could any woman say: "This is the Word of the Lord. Thanks be to God"?' she cried, hurling Melinda's Bible through the air.

'Alas, throughout the Old Testament, God's faithfulness is frequently contrasted with the moral decline of the Israelites,' commented Melinda as she retrieved her Bible.

'But, as far as the writer was concerned, it was clearly the plan to rape the male guest that was so abhorrent, the host and the Levite's callous selfishness and indifference to women's suffering was quite acceptable,' said Christobel bitterly.

'Which shows that the Bible arose in a patriarchal culture in which women were oppressed and marginalized,' commented Wade.

'You know, the Council of Chalcedon affirmed in 451 that Jesus Christ was fully divine *and* fully human,' said Ruth quietly, 'but Christians nearly always seem to focus on his divinity rather than his humanity. A sort of one-sided perspective has prevailed that sees him as Lord and saviour, the triumphant second person of the Trinity, not a real human being with human limitations. I wonder if it is the same with the Bible. We are often so intent on seeing it as the words of God, that we overlook that it is the words of men, and therefore subject to human limitations and mistakes.'

'*Also* the words of men – or *just* the words of men?' asked Liz.

'I'm still trying to work that one out,' admitted Ruth. 'I have a friend who has ended up rejecting the Bible altogether and leaving the Church, on the grounds that Christianity is irredeemably sexist and oppressive to women. However, there are liberating traditions within the Bible, and no one that I know of has ever been able to attribute a sexist statement to Jesus! So one of the reasons why I am doing this course is to try to get a better understanding of the Bible, to see how it can still be considered revelation.'

'Great!' said Liz. 'I suspect that all of us who've entered or been brought up in the Christian tradition have to wrestle with this issue sooner or later.'

'Of course the Bible's revelation!' declared Frank impatiently. 'It says so itself. 2 Timothy 3:16: "All Scripture is God-breathed [which means inspired] and is useful for teaching, rebuking, correcting and training in righteousness".'

'That verse is the classic justification for a fundamentalist interpretation of the Bible,' said Wade with a sigh. 'It has to be, as it's the only place in the Bible where inspiration is directly mentioned. But there is no reference whatsoever to inerrancy; "useful" is not a synonym for "absolutely necessary"; and "all Scripture" doesn't refer to modern Bibles because the canon hadn't been closed then. Fundamentalists claim far more for the Bible than the biblical writings do. There is no evidence, for example, that Jesus went around saying: "Read my lips. I am giving you inspired, inerrant, authoritative teaching that will be valid for all time. You'd better believe it or else." And while he certainly valued the Old Testament writings, he didn't rigidly stick to them but was extremely critical of the scribes and Pharisees who did! I could go on and on. Paul's letters reveal that he changed his mind on a number of issues, and he admitted that he could not always speak for the Lord and that his knowledge was limited. If you don't believe me, read 1 Corinthians 13:9: "For we know only in part, and we prophesy only in part ... For now we see in a mirror dimly ..." If you ask me, Paul would have been horrified if he had known that two thousand years down the track his letters to particular Christian communities (dealing with particular issues that concerned them) would be regarded as the infallible, inerrant, timeless revelation of God to humankind!'

'And I must say that I can't see how parts of the Old Testament are useful for "training in righteousness",' said Maureen. 'A few weeks ago there was nothing on TV but sex and violence, so I decided to spend an evening reading the Bible instead. I sat myself down in the chair with the cat on my lap and a packet of chocolate éclairs and started off with Genesis. Talk of sex and violence! It made the soap operas on TV look tame!'

'Yeah, I used to think that the Bible must be really pious and boring,' said Jason enthusiastically, 'but then I stumbled across Song of Songs!'

Melinda pursed her lips disapprovingly.

'Would anyone who hasn't had a chance to speak like to say something now?' intervened Liz with a smile. She looked at Kirsty, Dave, and me. 'Have you any thoughts on the Bible?'

Kirsty confessed that she had never actually read the Bible from cover to cover. She had probably read most of the New

Testament, but apart from hearing stories about Noah's ark, Jonah and the whale, etc. at Sunday School, she didn't know much about the Old Testament.

'But I suppose that I've always sort of thought … I mean, I just sort of accepted that the Bible is true. It is, isn't it?' she ended on a rather confused and anxious note.

'What is truth?' replied Wade with a wave of his hand.

'Something's either true or it's false, and as the Bible is the Word of God, and God is truth, it must be true,' insisted Frank.

'But are "true" and "false" always that clear cut?' asked Liz. 'What if I said to you: "It's a lovely day today." Is that true?'

'It's raining,' retorted Maureen. 'And I forgot my umbrella. And when this finishes I'll have to wait an hour for my bus, and then go home to tackle a mountain of washing which I can't put outside to dry because it's too wet, and there'll be no one to talk to except the cat. What's so lovely about that?'

'Oh, I'll drive you home,' exclaimed Christobel, 'and on the way we'll stop at an absolutely gorgeous little coffee shop that I've discovered and have a cup of coffee and a chat. The washing can wait!'

'Well, that would be nice,' acknowledged Maureen gratefully.

'So, even if the weather is awful, it can be a lovely day if something pleasant happens,' remarked Liz.

'I rather think, Liz, that that example just goes to show how grateful we should be that God has provided us with objective truth in the Bible, truth which is sure and certain whatever our individual circumstances,' said Melinda.

'OK. An example from the Bible,' said Liz. 'Psalm 91 – is it true?'

'Yes,' affirmed Frank and Melinda at once.

'Last year I had a bit of a health scare,' said Ruth slowly. 'I thought that I might have cancer, and although I tried not to worry, deep down I was really quite afraid. The day I had to go into hospital for the biopsy I opened up my Bible and the words of Psalm 91 seemed to leap off the page straight at me, just as if God was talking to me: "I will cover you with my pinions, and under my wings you will find refuge ... You will not fear the terror of the night, or the arrow that flies by day, or the pestilence that stalks in the darkness ..." Sure enough, the biopsy showed that nothing sinister was wrong.'

'But lots of Christians do get cancer and suffer and die,' Jason pointed out. 'So how can Psalm 91 be true for them?'

'They just need to have faith,' maintained Frank.

'But that doesn't guarantee automatic healing,' argued Christobel. 'Troubles and tragedies can cause real faith crises.'

'Especially when people think that psalms like Psalm 91 should be taken literally,' said Liz with a nod, 'although, I must admit, few people take Psalm 91 so literally that they go around stamping on deadly snakes, confident that they won't harm them because it says so in verse 13!'

'That's the trouble with fundamentalists,' said Wade dryly. 'They don't take the Bible literally enough!'

'I tell you what, I'll bring Deidre along one week so that you can practise,' Jason told Frank and Melinda.

'Is she poisonous?' asked Kirsty, wide-eyed.

'No, but she wouldn't take very kindly to being stamped on,' Deidre's owner cheerfully responded.

'The point that I am trying to make,' interjected Liz, 'is that "truth" is not always a straightforward concept, the opposite to "falsehood", especially with regard to the Bible. It may be difficult for many people who are not cured of an illness, or protected from danger, to appreciate that Psalm 91 is "true". However, other people have such strong faith in God that

Psalm 91 can give them comfort and hope, regardless of what happens to them. It assures them that God cares for them. And Psalm 91 is just one example. Much of the Bible consists of poetry, myths, legends, metaphors, and so on, that are not literally, historically, factually accurate but may point to a deeper, more profound meaning which we believe is "true".'

'And we can seriously distort Scripture and fall into idolatry if we insist on taking some things literally,' said Wade. 'Saying that the Bible is "God's Word" is like saying that "God is our Father". "Father" and "Word" are both just figures of speech, metaphors. God is clearly not a male sexual being who copulates with a female sexual being to produce offspring, and the Bible is not a unit of language that was spat out of the divine mouth!'

'I am not sure how well that answers your question, Kirsty,' said Liz, 'but I am sure that we will be wrestling with this issue a lot more in the coming weeks!'

'By the sounds of things I'll be doing so much wrestling I'd better invest in a pair of those gloves that wrestlers wear!' said Maureen. 'Or am I getting confused with boxing? Do wrestlers wear gloves?'

'I don't know, but try instead getting a book like David Ord and Robert Coote's *Is the Bible True? Understanding the Bible Today* (SCM, 1994),' advised Liz. 'Or, if you prefer a more conservative guide, Gordon Fee and Douglas Stuart's *How to Read the Bible for All its Worth*, 2nd edition (Zondervan, 1993).'

At this point Dave got up and said that he was sorry but he had to leave to attend soccer practice, and Liz decided that we had all probably wrestled enough for one day.

On the way out I heard Melinda say to Frank that it was a pity that we had such a young and inexperienced tutor, who obviously didn't know what she was talking about. I'm afraid that Liz must have heard her, too. I know that she's also not too happy about the way things went. I found myself standing behind her in a queue in the refectory as she wailed to a friend: 'It's the tutorial group from hell!'

I trust that she was speaking metaphorically!

Week·Two

Approaching the Bible

We had an extra participant in the tutorial discussion to-day. Dave turned up with Otto. He is the biggest German Shepherd that I have ever seen: more the size of a pony than a dog. He bounded into the room, apparently very pleased to join us, and immediately leapt up at Melinda. She shrieked, I'm not sure whether from fright or the prospect of muddy paw prints on her cream skirt. Kirsty edged around the room to stand behind me. Liz, rather annoyed, begged Dave to restrain his pet.

'Sit! Sit!' yelled Dave, but Otto was too busy making the acquaintance of Maureen and Wade to take any notice.

'Sit! Sit!! Sit!!!' yelled Dave again. This time Otto realized that he was being addressed and lay over on his back and waved his paws in the air.

'Stay! Stay!' yelled Dave.

Otto gave ecstatic yelps as Wade rubbed his stomach with the tip of his shoe.

Dave explained that Otto was on his way to soccer practice with him and wouldn't be any trouble.

'Couldn't you have left him in the car?' demanded Liz.

'He doesn't like being left in cars on his own,' explained Dave. 'He gets bored and chews the seats.'

'Well, as long as he is good he can stay,' conceded Liz

reluctantly. 'Now, can we begin by naming some of the ways in which we can approach the Bible today?'

'We should always begin with prayer,' replied Melinda firmly. 'We should ask God to make the meaning of a passage clear. What can we learn from this passage? How can we apply it to our lives? I meet with a group of Christians from my church once a week for Bible study and I am finding it extremely beneficial.'

Someone walked along the corridor outside our tutorial room and Otto almost deafened us with his barking.

'Quiet! Quiet!' shouted Dave, jumping up to shut the door.

Otto gave one final bark and wandered behind Kirsty.

'I'm trying to get up at six o'clock each morning so that I can spend an hour reading the Bible and praying,' revealed Kirsty, glancing over her shoulder uneasily, 'but some mornings it's awfully hard to wake up.'

'I should think so! Anyone who *voluntarily* gets up in the morning at that hour has to be crazy,' said Jason, leaning over to pat Otto. 'It isn't natural. Don't you agree old chap?'

Otto obligingly woofed.

'Mornings were always hectic in my house,' said Maureen, reminiscing. 'There was no time for reading the morning paper, let alone the Bible. There'd be Don wanting his bacon and eggs and his shirt ironed, and the kids' school lunches to pack, and the cat ...'

Otto started barking again and tearing around the room.

'Isn't he clever?' said Dave proudly. 'He knows what a you-know-what is.'

'Can he spell?' asked Maureen.

Dave didn't think that Otto was that advanced.

'Well, the C–A–T,' continued Maureen, 'would be demanding to be fed, and goodness knows what else would be happening. When everyone finally left and I had the house to myself I'd make myself a nice cup of tea and put my feet up for a few minutes. No time for Bible reading then, either, but I could have a quick chat with God and ask him for strength to get through the rest of the day.'

'Did you read the Bible any other time?' asked Liz.

Maureen shook her head.

'Every so often I'd feel guilty about not reading it more,' she admitted, 'but somehow I never found the time. My old mother, now – she used to read two chapters every night before she went to sleep, regular as clockwork, but by the time I got to bed I'd always be too tired to do that. Eyes would blur at the second verse so I gave up trying. Yes, you can smell my latest C–A–T, can't you,' she added to Otto, who was sniffing her legs.

'My main contact with the Bible has always been at morning and evening prayer and Mass,' reflected Ruth, 'when I'd hear the specially selected readings. I suppose that they reinforced what I was brought up to assume: that Scripture is divine revelation, the source of Church doctrines and personal messages from God that somehow transcend time and culture.'

Liz wrote on the white board *Approach 1: the Bible as Divine Revelation*.

She then accidentally dropped the white board marker and Otto seized on it with delight. Dave rescued it and returned it to her, dripping with saliva. She screwed up her nose and wiped it with a tissue.

'But the biblical writings were written two to three thousand years ago,' objected Wade when Otto had settled down again. 'A vast time and cultural gap exists between the biblical world and the modern world. You can only maintain that the Bible transcends time and culture if you ignore the enormous strides that have been made in our understanding of the world in the last couple of centuries.'

'If believing the Bible is deemed to be a sign of ignorance, I am proud to be considered ignorant!' declared Melinda.

'Yeah, and we'll see on the Last Day who's right,' muttered Frank.

'As far as I'm concerned, the Bible is a collection of human writings which were written in particular historical periods,' said Wade, crossing his arms, 'and you can't understand them properly unless you study their historical background.'

Otto stuck his nose in Kirsty's bag and discovered her lunch. She let him have it, and one tuna sandwich was demolished in seconds.

'Wade has just brought up another approach to the Bible,' said Liz, writing on the board *Approach 2: the Bible as a Collection of Ancient Texts.* 'It certainly takes into account the time and cultural gap, and it has been the dominant approach among Protestant biblical scholars since the 1800s. The hierarchy of the Roman Catholic Church initially resisted it, but in an encyclical in 1943 Pope Pius XII permitted Catholic scholars to use modern historical methods. Using such methods, scholars seek to find out as much as possible about the authors of biblical writings, the oral and written sources that they might have drawn on, the people who they were writing for, the culture that they lived in, and so on. The primary aim is not to find out what God may be revealing to us *now*, but to discover what the writers originally wanted to say.'

'And the end result just seems to be a mass of negative, destructive, conflicting theories,' complained Melinda.

Before anyone could respond Otto broke wind. Dave rushed to open a window, shut because of the air conditioning. He couldn't get it up, and had to open the door instead.

'It certainly has been difficult to get agreement among scholars on some historical issues,' admitted Liz with a handkerchief over her nose, 'and much remains uncertain which can be very frustrating. That is partly why there has been greater interest lately in a literary approach to the Bible.'

She wrote *Approach 3: the Bible as a Literary Work of Art* on the board, explaining as she did that those who follow this approach regard the Bible as a piece of literature which can be studied as you would any other great literary classic. Scholars examine things like the narrative plot of a passage, the way characters are developed, the imagery that is used, the author's style, etc. The aim is to put aside whatever historical world might lie behind the text and try to enter imaginatively into the 'story world' of the text.

Some poor person walked along the corridor, not expecting to be accosted by an enormous German Shepherd bounding through a seminar room door. It took Dave some time to restrain Otto, pick up the books which the victim had dropped, and apologize.

'But the Bible is not just a great literary classic: it is sacred Scripture!' insisted Melinda when order was more or less restored.

'And the only true way to approach it is with a humble heart,' maintained Frank, 'so that God can reveal the meaning to us.'

'But no matter how humble we try to be, we cannot read the Bible without interpreting it,' said Wade, 'and just as with any other artistic work, we all have different opinions/viewpoints/prejudices. I bet that if we all went to see a film, or a play, or a display at the art gallery, and then got together afterwards to discuss it, we would find that it had affected us all differently. What appealed to me may not have appealed to Melinda, and so on.'

'Did you read in the paper about that painting that was sold for hundreds of thousands of pounds a few weeks ago?' demanded Maureen. 'Real bizarre it was. I remember saying to my best friend Enid, I wouldn't put that thing above my mantelpiece if you paid me! Horrible and depressing it was, and yet art critics rave about it. Otto, I know that I shouldn't make personal comments, but your breath stinks.'

'It is irrelevant whether we *like* the Bible or not,' said Melinda impatiently. 'The Bible is the Word of God regardless of our personal opinions.'

'But the way we read and understand it *is* affected by who we are, what our educational and cultural background is, and so on,' said Liz. 'We are all inclined to think that our interpretation is the only right and obvious one, but the truth is, people do interpret Scripture differently – so what strikes me as obvious may be totally incomprehensible to someone else!'

'It's the same with lots of things,' contributed Christobel. 'Take my garden, for instance. Only yesterday an old school friend whom I haven't seen for years dropped in and we went out to the garden. Now, I absolutely adore my little garden. It's not much bigger than a tennis court, but I've planted several lovely trees and shrubs and lots of annuals and bulbs. There's a pond with a cute little fountain and a waterfall, a bird-bath and a bird-feeder, and a dear little stone wall and garden seat. When I usher visitors out the back door for the first time I wait for them to stop in surprise and say: "Oh, Christobel, what a lovely garden!" Well, yesterday we went out to the garden and Erica stopped and said: "Oh, Christobel, you've got room for a tennis court!" Come to think of it, we never were very close.'

'I know just how you feel, dear,' said Maureen. 'I've got a sister-in-law who lives on a farm. Every so often she descends for a visit. I don't know why she does, because she spends most of her time complaining about the traffic fumes and crowds in the city. And she brings half the farm with her: dozens of eggs straight from the hen house (covered in you-know-what) and gallons of milk straight from the cow, and I'm supposed to be on a low cholesterol diet! What got me on to that? Oh, yes, the garden. Before my lovely old home was sold (because of the divorce, you know), I used to be real proud of my back garden, but do you think that Mavis would admire it? She was always too busy saying what a pity it was I didn't have room for fruit trees and a vegetable patch, and couldn't I get Don to buy me a decent permanent clothes line instead of that fold-away thing?'

'Of course, one of the great contributions of feminist scholarship has been the way feminist scholars have shown that there is no such thing as objective scholarship,' asserted Wade, ignoring Maureen.

Christobel absolutely agreed. 'Whereas most scholars in the past were boring, white, middle-class, middle-aged, European or North American males who assumed that *their* way of looking at the world was the only one, now, at long last, feminists are reading the Bible from *women's* perspectives,' she exclaimed.

Liz added *Approach 4: the Bible as Interpreted from a Particular Perspective* to the list. She then put her white board marker back on the table and Otto reached up and grabbed it. 'Oh, he can have it if it will keep him quiet,' she told Dave as he unsuccessfully tried to prise apart Otto's jaws.

'But isn't there a great danger that people can use the "there's no such thing as objective scholarship" argument as an excuse for reading into the Bible whatever they want to find?' asked Melinda. 'And feminists certainly do not speak for all women. None of my friends will have anything to do with feminism.'

' "Feminism" is a term which also means different things to different people,' said Liz with a wry smile. 'One of my favourite definitions of a feminist is someone who has discovered that women make up half the human race. But getting back to your point, I agree, Melinda, that a feminist cannot speak for all women. However, a characteristic of feminist scholarship is that feminists usually come clean, admit what their perspective is, and consciously interpret the Bible from that perspective. Likewise, some scholars strive to interpret the Bible from the perspective of "the poor", racial minority groups, etc. *Please*, Jason, don't throw the pen. Otto is too big a dog for this sized room,' she begged as Otto knocked over a chair in an excited attempted to fetch it.

'Sit! Sit!' yelled Dave, as ineffectually as ever.

'I should also say that scholars often combine approaches,' continued Liz in a resolute tone. 'Someone may adopt an historical/feminist or a literary/feminist approach, for example, but usually one approach predominates. You'll each have to choose one for your essay. But perhaps we should now get back to the historical approach. It embraces a number of methods known as "criticisms". Can you name some?'

'Textual criticism,' replied Jason. 'None of the original, first ever, manuscripts of biblical writings survive: Genesis by Moses, 1 Corinthians by Paul, the Ten Commandments by God, etc. Pity, because they'd be worth a fortune, wouldn't they, Otto? Somehow or other they've all been lost. The ancient Israelites and early Christians must have been awfully careless. As a result, we've only got copies and fragments of copies, and they contain heaps of differences in wording, so textual critics have to try to work out what is most likely to have been the original wording.'

Otto lay down and closed his eyes.

'They're just like kids, aren't they?' said Maureen. 'It's so nice and peaceful when they're asleep. You know, I've still got the King James Bible my mother gave me on my tenth birthday and it's quite different in lots of places from the Good

21

News Bible my kids got when they went to Sunday School. "He restoreth my soul; he leadeth me in the paths of righteousness for his name's sake" becomes "He gives me new strength, He guides me in the right paths, as he has promised".'

'That raises the issue of different translations,' responded Liz. 'Few people can read the Bible in the original languages that it was written in. Most of us have to rely on translations, and all translations are actually interpretations. The translator has to decide which word in English best conveys the original Greek or Hebrew, and often the Greek or Hebrew has several different meanings or nuances which cannot be effectively conveyed in English. Some translators try to be as faithful as possible to the original language, while others set out to make their translation as easy to understand as possible. It's fine if you want to use one of the most readable modern versions like the Good News Bible or the Contemporary English Version for devotional purposes, or the seventeenth-century King James if you love its poetry and "thees" and "thous", but you'll find that a lot of scholars use the Revised Standard Version, or the New Revised Standard Version. I'd recommend you get a copy of that if you haven't already, but it is also a good idea to have several translations on hand so that you can compare them.'

Otto began to snore.

'OK. Any other criticisms?' asked Liz.

'Source criticism,' replied Wade. 'Discerning the different "sources" which were available to the redactor.'

'The what?' asked Maureen.

'"Redactor" is sort of scholarly jargon for the writer/editor who, drawing on different sources, put a biblical book together in the form in which we have it now,' answered Liz. 'In New Testament study source criticism has been extremely important with regard to the gospels. For example, it is now widely accepted that Matthew and Luke used Mark as a source. In Old Testament study the Pentateuch has been the focus of source criticism. You all know what I mean by "Pentateuch"?'

Maureen and Kirsty looked blank.

'The first five books of the Bible (Genesis, Exodus, Leviticus, Numbers and Deuteronomy) which are called the Torah or Law by Jews,' explained Liz. 'It is now widely accepted that the Pentateuch is made up of four major literary sources which were written at different times in Israel's history. The first writer may have been a scribe at the court of King David or King Solomon in the tenth century BCE. He seems to have written a history of the Israelites from the perspective of the court, and he used the divine name "Yahweh" so he is called the Yahwist (or Jahwist). The second writer, known as the Elohist because he called God "Elohim", is thought to have lived in about the ninth century BCE, after Solomon's kingdom was divided into the northern kingdom (Israel) and the southern kingdom (Judah). He wrote from the perspective of the northern kingdom. After the fall of Israel in 722, the two histories, known as J and E, may have been put together. In the seventh century the Deuteronomists came onto the scene. They probably lived during the religious reforms which took place in King Josiah's reign, when worship was centralized in Jerusalem and new laws were created, and they promoted these changes in their writing. Finally, after the southern kingdom fell in 587 BCE, priests in exile in Babylon recorded details of Israelite worship and religious traditions, and put together their writing (P) with J, E, and D to form the Pentateuch as we know it now.'

'But Moses wrote the Pentateuch, the Bible says so,' said Frank, looking dumbfounded.

'And Jews and Christians have accepted that for centuries,' added Melinda curtly. 'Jesus himself clearly believed that Moses was the author so we cannot believe the four-source theory without believing that Christ is capable of error!'

'Jesus never set out to give a lecture on the authorship of the Pentateuch,' retorted Wade. 'His audience would have assumed that Moses was the author, and he had many more important points to make than to quibble about that. But I do not see why we cannot believe that he also accepted the assumptions of his generation. He clearly did not have the benefit of recent biblical scholarship.'

'In that case he was fortunate!' Melinda struck back. 'From what I have read, there have been numerous different versions of the four-source theory, different dates for J, E, D and P, and different theories about how they came together, and they are all highly inconclusive and just lead to endless controversies among scholars who should have better things to do with their time.'

'The four-source theory has certainly been questioned and modified over time, and it is still only a theory, not proven fact, but it has been widely accepted by biblical scholars,' Liz pointed out.

'And it is not just the Pentateuch that is composed of different sources,' said Wade. 'Read 1 Samuel 16 and 17 sometime. In chapter 16 King Saul is troubled by an evil spirit and he sends his servants to find a musician who can soothe him. One of them recommends David who comes to Saul's court and enters his service. Saul loves him dearly and makes him his armour bearer. In chapter 17, however, David is back home tending his father's sheep in Bethlehem and taking food to his brothers in Saul's army. On one of his visits to his brothers he hears the talk about Goliath and, after being

mocked by his brother as a mere shepherd boy (a strange atti-
tude to take toward the king's armour bearer), he kills Goliath
with his sling and stone. Then Saul demands to know who he
is: "Whose son is this youth?"!'

'David probably didn't spend long at Saul's court the first
time they met, and Saul didn't get to know much about him,'
explained Frank.

'Or Saul may simply have been incredulous at David's
courage and asked who he was as a rhetorical question,'
suggested Melinda. 'It is quite easy to resolve seeming contradictions like these.'

'It is a lot easier if you accept that two separate traditions
about how David and Saul met circulated in Israelite folk-
lore,' declared Wade, 'and the writer of 1 Samuel tried to put
them together.'

'When stories are passed on down the generations without
getting put into writing it's easy for different versions to come
about,' commented Maureen. 'I remember being told when I
was a kid that great-grandfather from Kent quarrelled with
his parents and ran away from home. He ended up on a ship
which was going to Australia. When the ship was just out of
Port Adelaide the captain was too drunk to steer it in safely,
so brave great-grandfather knocked him unconscious and
took over. Once the ship was safely docked great-grandfather
realized that he might be accused of mutiny, so he jumped
overboard and ran through the streets of Adelaide, pausing
only to grab some peas from the front of a shop. He then hid
in bushland in the hills behind Adelaide for three days until
he could see the ship sailing away. Now, as far as I am concerned, that's what happened, but a couple of years ago I
went to a reunion with some of my cousins and we all told
what we thought was great-grandfather's story. Every version
was different! Someone reckoned it was beans that he

grabbed; another was sure it was three weeks, not three days that he spent in the hills. Christobel, is that your leather bag that Otto is chewing?'

Unnoticed by us, Otto had woken up.

With a startled scream Christobel grabbed her bag. She surveyed with dismay the teeth marks while Dave shouted, 'Bad Dog! Bad Dog!'

Otto wagged his tail.

'So it is easy to understand how someone writing hundreds of years after Saul and David could find the details a bit confusing,' Liz said to Maureen.

'Only if you overlook the fact that the biblical writers were guided by the Holy Spirit,' maintained Melinda. 'I hardly think that there can be any comparison between the story of David and Saul and that of your ancestor, Maureen.'

'I think that it's awfully relevant,' declared Christobel, putting down her damaged bag and rushing to Maureen's defence, 'because stories must have been passed on orally in Israel and Judah, just like in other ancient cultures. The Bible didn't fall down from heaven intact, you know. I think that it's awfully fascinating to consider how it came into being.'

'Fascinating! It's just picking the Bible to bits, that's what it's doing,' grumbled Frank. ' "J wrote this and P wrote that …" And it's all totally unnecessary because God wrote the Bible and he preserved it in the form he wanted us to have it.'

Dave agreed that scholars seem to be going overboard dissecting and analysing the Bible. 'What's left at the end, that's what I want to know,' he asked. 'It's like if I got a car and pulled it to bits. I'd end up with a garage full of nuts and bolts and wheels and things, which might be very interesting if you like car parts, but there'd be no actual car for me to drive. So what's the point?'

'There isn't any point. Much biblical scholarship is just

unchristian, negative, and destructive,' lamented Melinda. 'All it does is destroy people's faith!'

'Their faith must be pretty shallow, then,' said Wade. 'It is essential that faith be well-informed. One of the reasons why so many people have left the Church in recent years (or can't be bothered joining) must be the fact that they cannot reconcile their experience of the modern world with simplistic belief in the Bible's timelessness and inerrancy. The Bible just seems meaningless and irrelevant. It is vitally important that the Church rescues the Bible from fundamentalism and uses it in ways that don't destroy the Church's credibility.'

'In my experience it is churches which preach the Bible which are growing in numbers,' proclaimed Melinda, 'not the ones with wishy-washy liberal ideas!'

'That is because in an age of great uncertainty people often want certainty,' responded Wade, 'and fundamentalism can give them that for a while. But if they begin to question what they are being taught and start thinking for themselves they soon discover that it is all a con and they are likely to end up worse off than before.'

'Now, you listen here ...' began Frank angrily.

He was interrupted by Otto barking at another unfortunate person walking past the door.

'I certainly come from a church which is declining in numbers,' said Maureen. 'You can count the number of people under fifty on one hand. And I've never heard my minister say that the Pentateuch wasn't written by Moses, or that there might have been different traditions about David and Saul, and all that. But, come to think about it, he hardly ever mentions the Old Testament in his sermons at all.'

'I think priests and ministers must face a great dilemma when they leave the seminary or theological college and start having to preach to congregations,' mused Ruth. 'How much of their new knowledge can they pass on without causing too much hurt and offence? It must be easy to lapse back into fairly simplistic Bible teaching.'

'Do we have to make a choice between belief in Scripture and learning?' asked Liz. 'Faith or education? Is there not a middle way?'

'There can be no middle ground when the so-called "learning" is so patently anti-christian,' declared Melinda.

'Is it anti-christian to respect the Bible so much that you want to find out as much as possible about how it came into being?' demanded Wade. 'Is it anti-christian to try to understand what the Bible is actually saying? Is it anti-christian to try to show how the Bible can be meaningful today?'

'It just doesn't seem right to criticize the Bible,' ventured Kirsty.

'But "critical" biblical scholarship is not necessarily critical in the usual negative sense of the word, Kirsty,' said Liz earnestly. 'It is derived from the Greek word *krinein* which means "to judge or discern". It is all about making intelligent, carefully-reasoned, and well-informed judgements about the Bible.'

'And feminist scholarship is not all negative either,' added Christobel, 'which is frightfully exciting. When I became a feminist a few years ago I really went off the Bible because it was so obviously biased against women, but the other day I was reading about Elizabeth Schussler Fiorenza, one of the great feminist biblical scholars. She certainly starts off with a hermeneutics of suspicion, the suspicion that all biblical writings are written from a male perspective which assumes and seeks to perpetuate male dominance. However, she also uses a hermeneutics of proclamation (assessing which texts are suitable for use in worship), a hermeneutics of remembrance (seeking women's stories that may be buried in the Bible and highlighting them), and a hermeneutics of creative actualization (helping women reclaim Bible stories through imagination, ritual, and art). Isn't that thrilling? No, you can't have my bag again, Otto, you naughty dog!'

'What on earth does "hermeneutics" mean?' asked Maureen, patting Otto.

'It is from the Greek word for interpretation,' answered Liz. 'You might have come across the notion of a "hermeneutical circle": readers bring to a written text their pre-understandings and prejudgements, and these shape the way they question and interpret the text. However, the text can also challenge their pre-understandings and prejudgements, and lead to different questions. So hopefully a sort of "hermeneutical spiral" emerges. Does that make sense?'

Kirsty's eyes looked rather glazed over but we all nodded.

'Another word that you will come across is "exegesis",' continued Liz. 'It is from the Greek *exegeomai* which means to "lead out of"…'

Otto leapt up at her excitedly and then tore around the room.

'He's looking for his L–E–A–D,' said Dave proudly, 'he thinks that you are going to take him for a W–A–L–K.'

'Sorry, Otto, no luck. As I was trying to say before Otto went berserk, exegesis means to L–E–A–D out or read out the meaning of a text. An exegesis of a passage is therefore an interpretation or explanation of it. Note that I said *an* interpretation, not *the* interpretation. Hayes and Holladay make a very important point in their book *Biblical Exegesis: A Beginner's Handbook*. We can never claim that any exegesis that we do will be *the* one and only true exegesis of a passage. Exegesis is always an ongoing process. One of the wonderful things about the Bible is that you can read a passage hundreds of times and something different may still strike you about it.'

'I like the way that Hayes and Holladay say that "exegesis does not allow us to master the text so much as it enables us to enter into it",' said Ruth.

'That's a great way to put it,' agreed Liz. 'I know that textual criticism and source criticism, and all the other criticisms that you will come across later, may seem intimidating now (and quite shocking and upsetting if you are used to thinking of the Bible as if dropped down from heaven intact), but I hope that in the long run they will help you "enter into" the text and appreciate it better. We are very privileged to live in a time when we can draw on so much biblical scholarship.'

'Even if a lot of it's contradictory and confusing?' said Melinda with a forced smile.

'Read a biblical text as respectfully, openly, honestly, questioningly, and prayerfully as you can,' advised Liz. 'Try to be aware of your own biases. Don't just seek to have them confirmed, but be prepared to let the text challenge you. Ponder it. Mull over it. Then read a selection of Bible dictionaries, handbooks, and commentaries which give scholars' different interpretations of the text. Decide which interpretation seems the most convincing to you. Always, of course, ask to be guided by the Holy Spirit. That won't ensure that you'll always come up with the right answers, but you may discover some insights about yourself, God, or the world which are incredibly profound.'

For once Melinda was silenced.

The same could not be said for Otto who took violent exception to another hapless individual going past the door. Dave said that perhaps he and Otto should get going to soccer practice, and Liz, massaging her temples with her finger tips, agreed that it was time to finish up.

'Have you got a headache, dear?' asked Maureen sympathetically. 'Would you like a painkiller? I always keep some in my bag. You never know when you might need one.'

Taking two, Liz agreed.

Week·Three

In the Beginning

There was no sign of Dave or Otto this week, which I must admit was a bit of a relief. However, Jason was the last to arrive, and he walked into the room carrying a canvas bag which *twitched*. I distinctly saw it. Kirsty noticed it too. Jason caught sight of our stares, opened the bag, and out slithered . . . Deidre!

Kirsty screamed.

'It's all right, she won't hurt you. She just wants to be friends,' assured Jason as Deidre lunged toward Liz. Liz took a step backwards, and said that this was supposed to be a Scripture tutorial, not a zoo.

'But Deidre wanted to come along,' insisted Jason. 'She wanted to make sure that no one was going to say any nasty, untrue things about the snake in Genesis. Didn't you, Deidre?'

Deidre turned to him and began to crawl underneath his jacket.

'Now she feels rejected. It's a terrible thing to be a snake with an inferiority complex.'

'Call me a coward if you like, but I refuse to stay in the same room with that thing,' Melinda told Liz as she edged past Jason towards the door.

'I knew that it was a good idea to bring her,' said Jason, looking pleased.

'Jason, could you please put Deidre back in the bag until the tutorial is over,' said Liz rather desperately, as Melinda prepared to go off in a huff. 'Then those who want to . . . er . . . meet her can afterwards, and those who don't can leave. We really must get started. We've got a lot to get through.'

Jason reluctantly unwound Deidre from his torso and guided her back into her bag which he put at his feet, underneath the table.

'You're sure that it can't get out?' demanded Maureen.

Jason said that *she* couldn't, and she wouldn't want to anyway, because we had hurt her feelings.

'How can you tell whether a snake is male or female?' asked Wade curiously.

Jason began to explain the indignity which Deidre had been subjected to in the interests of establishing her sex.

'You were asked to read Chapters 1–11 in Genesis, the first book in the Bible,' overrode Liz in a determined tone. 'So what kind of literature is 1–11?'

'History, of course,' said Frank.

'Yeah, history,' said Jason. 'History with sea monsters and talking snakes and miraculous trees and divine sons of God mating with daughters of humans to produce goodness-knows-what.'

'The supernatural elements are no problem for a believer,' stated Frank. 'Nothing is impossible to God!'

'If Jesus Christ and Paul were historical individuals, we must accept that Adam, Eve, and Noah were,' maintained Melinda.

'Why?' asked Wade.

'Because Jesus refered to Noah in Matthew 24,' responded Melinda, 'and Paul to Adam in Romans 5.'

'"Just as one man's trespass led to condemnation for all, so

33

one man's act of righteousness leads to justification and life for all",' quoted Frank with a pleased expression.

'The fact that Jesus and Paul might have assumed that Adam and Noah were historical figures doesn't mean that they really were,' sighed Wade. 'We've been through all this before.'

'You're denying the authority of the New Testament!' cried Melinda.

'No, just trying to point out that the New Testament writers lived in a certain historical period and their understanding of the world reflects the thought and culture of that period. We live in a different period and have a different understanding of how the world came into being. Genesis 1 is a classic example of an ancient creation story that is no longer binding today. Surely no one still believes that there is a great mass of water above us, separated from us by a dome of sky, on which is placed the sun, moon, and stars! But that is clearly what the ancient writer of Genesis 1 assumed:

> And God said, "Let there be a dome in the midst of the waters, and let it separate the waters from the waters." So God made the dome and separated the waters that were under the dome from the waters that were above the dome. And it was so. God called the dome Sky . . .'

'The upper waters could have been rain clouds,' suggested Melinda.

'Or there really could have been water, which was up above somewhere until it came down in the Flood,' said Frank.

'Yeah, the Flood!' said Jason. 'I've always been fascinated by the Flood! How did Noah get hold of two of every kind of bird and animal? The koalas and kangaroos from Australia and the kiwis from New Zealand had a pretty long way to travel to get to the ark! The poor things would have been half dead by the time they got there. And just think how much water it would have taken to cover *all* the mountain ranges in the world – even Mount Everest got submerged! Frank's just explained where the water came from, but where did it go afterward? We're talking about quite a few gallons, you know. It had to drain off somewhere . . .'

'I remember when I was doing my stint as a Sunday School teacher we had a lesson on Noah's ark,' remarked Maureen. 'I got this idea from a book for craft work. You get a circle of blue cardboard, fold it in half, and stand it up, and that makes the sea, and then you insert a little boat into the fold, and the boat rocks. The kids coloured in their boats, and stuck little fishes on their seas. Everyone had a great time except one little kid who was real upset about all the people and animals who drowned. She kept wanting to know how God could have let that happen.'

'I hope that you told her that the people were very wicked and sinful and deserved to die,' said Melinda.

'Yes, but she still thought that it was a horrible story, and the more I came to think about it, I realized that she was right! You spend weeks telling kids that God is love, and merciful and forgiving and all that, and then you go and talk about how he wiped out the entire human race except for one miserly family.'

'Of course, the flood story is only a myth,' said Wade coolly, 'and numerous versions of it circulated in the ancient Near East. The Atrahasis epic from Babylon includes a creation story as well. Some of the lower-class Igigi gods have to perform manual labour, and they get sick of this and go on strike. The upper-class Anunaki gods respond by killing the ringleader, but they mix his blood with clay to form humans

35

to do the menial tasks instead of the Igigi. However, the humans multiply rapidly, and they disturb the gods with their noise, so the gods decide to send a flood to wipe them out. Before this happens, one of the gods, Enki, warns his favourite human, Atrahasis, of the impending doom, and Atrahasis builds a boat to save his family and animals. They duly escape, but all other humans die. The gods then regret wiping out their labour force, and are quite pleased when Atrahasis turns up safe and can renew the human race.'

'That's a load of rubbish,' said Frank. 'Nothing like Genesis. It was sin, not noise, that made God decide to send the Flood . . .'

'Interestingly, in the Babylonian Gilgamesh epic,' continued Wade, 'the boat of the human survivor of the flood, Utnapishtim, lands on a mountain, and he sends out a succession of birds (a dove, a swallow, and a raven) until finally the raven doesn't return so that he knows that there must be dry land somewhere. Then, like Noah, he sacrifices some animals to the gods, and they smell the burning meat and crowd around like flies.'

'Such stories are clearly garbled versions of the Genesis account,' said Melinda dismissively.

'But scholars say they come from the early second millennium, hundreds of years *before* Genesis,' retorted Wade. 'It is much more likely that the writers of Genesis knew *them*.'

'That depends on when you date Genesis,' responded Melinda. 'If you believe the Bible, Moses would have written Genesis in a little after the middle of the second millennium, about 1450 BC, and he drew on much older traditions which were passed on down the generations of Israelites.'

'Adam lived more than 200 years after Methuselah was born,' calculated Frank, 'and he must have lived until Noah was about 600 years old, and then Noah would have lived until Terah's time, and Terah was Abraham's father, and Abraham would have lived to talk to Joseph, who would still have been alive when Amran was young; and Amran was still around when Moses was born, so it is quite easy to see how the true accounts of creation and the Flood could have been passed on . . .'

'You actually believe that people lived hundreds of years, like it says in Genesis?' asked Jason incredulously.

'Why not?' said Frank.

'God let the first humans live longer to get the human race started,' explained Melinda.

Well, I pity the poor things, then,' said Maureen. 'I wouldn't want to live 800 years. Think of all the great-great-great-great-great-great-grandchildren's birthdays you'd have to remember!'

'If you follow the chronology in Genesis, you end up with the universe being created in about 4000 BCE,' Wade pointed out with a sarcastic laugh. 'So how do you reconcile that, Melinda, with the widespread agreement among scientists that the universe originated about 15 billion years ago, the earth began to form about 4.6 billion years ago, and *Homo sapiens* emerged about 30 thousand to 40 thousand years ago. I admit that compared to the origins of the universe, humans are a fairly recent addition, but we've still been around a hell of a lot longer than six thousand years!'

'The "days" in which God created the world in Genesis 1 may refer to geological ages,' conceded Melinda, 'and the genealogies may only give the names of prominent ancestors. Many may have been left out.'

'Well, I'd rather trust the Word of God than scientists,' declared Frank adamantly. 'A scientist finds three or four old bones, and the next thing you know he's produced a picture of *Neo cranio erectus* someone-or-another, his wife, kids, and hut! And evolutionists think creationists are gullible!'

'Let's get one thing straight,' maintained Wade. 'It does not say anywhere in Genesis that Genesis was written by Moses, and it does not say that it was directly inspired by God. There is no "thus says the Lord"! The creation stories are clearly Israelite human reflection on the origins of the world, from the time of the monarchy in about the ninth or tenth century BCE, and the Babylonian exile in the sixth.'

'So you are postulating the existence of two different sources?' said Liz.

'Yes,' agreed Wade. 'There are clearly two different creation accounts. It doesn't take much in the way of brains to see that. Scholars usually attribute Genesis 2:4 – 3:24 to the Yahwist (J), writing in the ninth or tenth century, and Genesis 1:1 – 2:3 to the priestly writer (P) who wrote during the sixth-century exile.'

'But Genesis 2 and 3 is not another creation account,' protested Melinda. 'There is no mention of the creation of the sun, moon, stars, and so forth. It is just an expansion of Genesis 1, recapitulating the creation of the human race.'

'So how come plants and animals are created *before* humans in Genesis 1, and *afterwards* in Genesis 2?' demanded Jason.

'God provided Adam with the plants and animals in Genesis 2 which he had created in Genesis 1,' answered Frank.

'Oh, give me strength!' muttered Wade. 'There are not only differences in detail,' he asserted in his normal voice. 'There are also differences in style, terminology, and theological perspectives. In Genesis 1 the tone is formal, majestic, repetitious, and authoritative, whereas Genesis 2 is presented as a vivid story. In Genesis 1 God is referred to as "Elohim", and in

Genesis 2 as "Yahweh" or "Yahweh Elohim". In Genesis 1 "Elohim" is majestic, transcendent, and very much outside the universe which is being created; in Genesis 2 "Yahweh" is near and involved in the universe, making humans like a potter makes pots, walking in the garden, and so on. In Genesis 1 humans are created in the image of "Elohim"; in Genesis 2 it is stressed that they are created from the ground. The word "Adam" is actually a wordplay on the Hebrew word *adamah* which means ground.'

'And male and female are created simultaneously in Genesis 1, whereas the woman is created after the man in Genesis 2,' added Ruth.

'Not according to Phyllis Trible in her book *God and the Rhetoric of Sexuality*!' interjected Christobel, with eyes sparkling. 'Trible translates "Adam" as "earth creature" because there was no sexual differentiation until the creation of sexuality in 2:21–22. And she says that the woman wasn't created as the "helper" of the man, either, as a lot of translations say. "Companion" much better expresses the Hebrew word than helper, which can imply a sort of subordinate assistant. Trible shows how the man and the woman were created to live in mutuality and equality and find fulfilment in one another, to "become one flesh". But there have been the most dreadful misogynistic interpretations of Genesis 2–3, and frightful generalizations have been made. For centuries women have been accused of being "daughters of Eve", the wicked temptress who caused Adam to sin. But if you actually *read* the story, you can see that the woman was intelligent and independent. She was the spokesperson for the couple. She theologized with the snake and decided that she wanted to pursue knowledge rather than remain ignorant. Hence she ate the fruit of the tree of knowledge and generously shared it with her partner. Then, when God turned up, did the man bravely admit what he had done? No, he did not. He first tried to hide, and then he blamed the woman. Well, if being a daughter of Eve means being like the woman in this story, I am proud to be a daughter of Eve!'

On this passionate note Christobel collapsed back into her chair.

'I always did think that Adam was a bit of a wimp,' commented Maureen. 'All he cared about was his stomach. Typical male.'

'Trible's book is a very good example of a literary-feminist approach to the Bible,' said Liz with a smile.

'But we must not overlook one of the great truths of Genesis,' said Melinda firmly, 'the awful cost of disobeying God.'

'And the fact that Satan is always trying to trap God's people,' added Frank.

'The snake is not the embodiment of evil,' snapped Wade. 'And the Adam and Eve story is not about the origin of death in the world, either, because no one in the story actually dies. And it is not about a "Fall" from perfection, because there was never such a thing as perfection! The story is all about power and control. James Kennedy, in an article in the *Journal for the Study of the Old Testament* 47 (1990), points out that ancient creation stories functioned to legitimate social order and political power, and Genesis 2–3 clearly promotes the values of the Israelite monarchy. Yahweh is portrayed as a wealthy landowner who strolls in the garden in the evening. The first couple are peasants, with a duty to till the ground. The snake possibly represents dissident elements in society who were trying to incite rebellion by encouraging peasants to seek knowledge and pursue independent action, to question the status quo and break free of the ruling elite. As Kennedy says, "enforced ignorance is a technique of control. In accord with this ideology the Genesis garden story portrays peasant ignorance as natural, that is, as part of the created order". Consequently, the peasants' attempt to gain knowledge results in expulsion from the garden, and the curses of Genesis 3.'

'Kennedy's article is a good example of a historical approach to the Bible, using a socio-political analysis,' observed Liz.

'I read John Michael Perry's *Exploring the Genesis Creation and Fall Stories*,' said Ruth, 'and he suggests that the Yahwist might have been writing to warn King Solomon not to give in to the coaxing of his foreign wives to worship fertility gods. He says that handling serpents was part of those sorts of cults, as serpents were regarded as phallic symbols!'

'I don't think that Deidre would like to be considered a phallic symbol, any more than the embodiment of evil,' said Jason.

Kirsty shivered as she suddenly remembered Deidre's existence.

'And Perry's argument harks back to the absolutely appallingly widespread view that women are temptresses,' exclaimed Christobel. 'I think that Kennedy's interpretation makes more sense. And, while I think of it, I wanted to make a point about the curses in Genesis 3. You know, it is absolutely ridiculous, but some people have argued that women shouldn't be given anaesthetics when they are in labour because God wants women to suffer pain!'

'I bet they were men. If they had to endure two days of labour, like I did when Gail was born, they'd pretty quickly change their minds,' muttered Maureen. 'And what about that husbands ruling over wives rubbish in 3:16?'

'That's another verse that has been continually misogynistically misinterpreted,' cried Christobel. 'Male chauvinists are quick to point out that the Bible says that women should be subordinate, but they don't consider the full context: subordination is not the natural order of things that God intended from the beginning of time, but the result of sin. We should be trying to return to equality and mutuality, not accepting the sinful situation as it is . . . '

'And God took a step toward reconciliation with Adam and Eve by making clothes for them,' reflected Ruth. 'That's what I like about Genesis 1–11. There is the sin/punishment theme, but there is also grace and mitigation of punishment. God not only clothes Adam and Eve, but puts a protecting mark on Cain, and saves Noah and his family . . . '

'But are the stories myths or did they really happen?' burst out Kirsty, able to contain herself no longer.

'Of course they really happened,' said Frank. 'Myths are lies, and God never lies.'

'Yes, myths are either the superstitious beliefs held by credulous people or the weird and wonderful stories about gods used in primitive cultures to explain the world,' said Melinda disdainfully.

'Like Elohim creating the world in seven days,' said Jason with a grin.

'Six,' corrected Frank. 'He rested on the seventh.'

'Kirsty, I don't think that myths are necessarily untrue,' intervened Ruth quickly. 'They can reflect deep, profound reflection on perennial human questions, like what brought death, suffering, and sin into the world, and why we have aspirations toward immortality. However, I wonder whether Genesis 1 is actually *anti-myth*. I know that the author assumes that ancient cosmological beliefs are true, that there is water above the dome of the sky, and that sort of thing, but when you compare Genesis 1 to ancient Near Eastern creation myths there are lots of differences. Genesis 1 stresses that the sun, moon, and stars were all *created*, they are not deities in their own right that have to be worshipped. And creation is *good*, and under God's control. Fearsome chaos has been overcome by order. Above all, humans are created in the image of God, not to do menial tasks as in the Atrahasis myth, or to be subservient to any animals that might be worshipped as gods, but to have dominion over the natural world!'

'So if Genesis 1 is not myth, or scientific fact, what is it?' asked Liz.

'I like the way that Walter Brueggemann says on page 25 of his commentary on Genesis that it is "a theological and pastoral statement addressed to a real historical problem",' answered Ruth. 'During their exile in Babylon the Israelites must have succumbed at times to hopelessness and despair. But Genesis 1 is so positive. It affirms that God *is* in control. And I think that its message has a certain timelessness about it. In view of the enormous ecological crises that we face today, surely we need to cherish the understanding that creation is good. I am not comfortable with humans being given dominion over animals and told to subdue the earth. I can see how that idea could have been liberating in the ancient world when nature could have seemed fearsome, but today it can be an excuse for exploitation. However, if we accept that creation is a source of delight to the creator, in whose image we are made, shouldn't we delight in it too? And if we are the climax of God's creation, don't we have a great responsibility to care for the rest of creation?'

'Mmm. Actually, what I like about that creation story is that even God had to rest,' said Maureen. 'We all need times of relaxation and recreation. Last weekend I should have been doing housework and writing an essay, but I thought, 'Bother it. I'm going to take a day off.' And I did. I didn't even go to church. I slept in instead. Really enjoyed myself. I felt ever so much better afterward.'

'Maureen, I am sure that God did not *need* to rest,' said Melinda. 'He only did so to indicate to us that we should keep the Sabbath holy . . . '

'You mean by going to church, and only reading good Christian books, and not playing sport or doing any work?' asked Maureen. 'That's what my mother always insisted on. But I could never understand why "not doing any work" didn't mean that you didn't have to slave over the old wood stove to cook a roast dinner. And then when I discovered that Sunday wasn't the real Sabbath anyway, it made even less sense . . . '

'OK. Following the creation stories there is the story of Cain and Abel,' said Liz when she could get a word in, 'and that is traditionally ascribed to the Yahwist because it has a similar style, vocabulary, and theological perspective to Genesis 2–3. Likewise, Genesis 5 is ascribed to the priestly writer. But what about the flood narrative?'

'That's clearly a combination of J and P,' replied Wade, 'they're woven together.'

'Ridiculous!' sniffed Melinda.

'It's not ridiculous,' said Wade with another sigh. 'It is a theory which helps explain the discrepancies in the flood narrative, like why 7:17 says that the rains lasted 40 days, and 7:24 says 150 days!'

'It rained for 40 days, but the flood waters lasted for 150,' retorted Melinda.

'Well, how many of each kind of animal did Noah take into the ark?' asked Wade dryly. 'Two of each kind, like it says in 7:8, or seven like it says in 7:2?'

'As well as discrepancies in detail, there also seem to be different theological perspectives and different styles in the narrative,' ventured Ruth. 'The priestly writer was very precise about the measurements of the ark, and the dates when everything happened . . . '

'Boring!' interrupted Maureen.

'It is a bit,' said Ruth with a smile, 'but what I find more interesting is that, as in Genesis 1, he had a cosmic focus. His flood story is almost a reversal of the creation story. In Genesis 1 God makes order out of chaos, in the flood story chaos returns: "the fountains of the great deep burst forth". It doesn't just rain! Also God (called Elohim, I think) is majestic and transcendent, as in Genesis 1. However, in the Yahwist account God (Yahweh) is much more human. When he sees how wicked people are he is "grieved to his heart" and sorry that he has made them . . . '

'Just like a kid throwing a tantrum!' said Maureen. '"I'm not going to come out to play with you today, and you're not my best friend any more . . . "'

Melinda was stunned that Maureen should take such a serious subject so lightly, but Ruth agreed that it did seem a bit like a divine tantrum. 'Fortunately, as the story goes, Yahweh gets over it, and decides that even though humans are thoroughly inclined to evil, he will never again try to blot them out. The priestly writer, on the other hand, finishes up with a formal agreement or covenant, the sign of which was the rainbow.'

'But did the Flood really happen or is it just a story?' asked Kirsty, perplexed.

'I think that the whole of Genesis 1–11 is not history but theology,' replied Ruth, 'reflection on the nature of God, and our relationship with God.'

'But if there are different theological perspectives . . . ?' wondered Kirsty aloud.

'It shows that there must have been different theological traditions in circulation in ancient Israel,' Ruth responded eagerly. 'The final editor didn't try to suppress all the differences, which was wonderfully honest of him, I think. It isn't surprising that there are differences. Even today different churches have different understandings of God. We are all still grappling to understand. My favourite definition of theology is "faith seeking understanding". Theology is about seeking, it is not about having all the answers.'

'Which is real frustrating at times,' said Maureen. 'What I can't understand, and wish that I could, is how can God let evil happen? I know that poor old Adam and Eve usually get the blame for bringing evil into the world, but who put the tree of the knowledge of good and evil (or whatever it was called) into the garden? God. Who created the snake? God. So isn't God ultimately responsible? And it was downright wrong of Cain to murder his brother Abel, no denying that, but he was provoked into doing it because God unfairly preferred Abel's offering to Cain's. I can understand Cain getting upset. As a mother, I've always tried to make sure that I treated all my kids equal. God failed a basic parenting test there! It strikes me that whenever there's pain, suffering, and evil in the Bible, God's up to his neck in it.'

'This is one of the perennial human questions, isn't it?' mused Ruth. 'Where is God in the midst of evil? But isn't one of the messages of the Cross the fact that God is up to God's neck in pain, suffering, and evil?'

'You have to remember, Maureen, that Scripture tells us that God created angels,' lectured Melinda, 'but some of them rebelled against God and set out to destroy his work. One of them, Satan, is the ruler of the darkness of this world, and since Adam sinned in the Garden of Eden man has been slave to Satan . . . '

As Melinda was talking I felt something wrap itself around my ankle. I froze, then forced myself to look underneath the table. It was Deidre's tail end. I suppose that it could have been worse. It could have been her head end. I soon discovered where that was. Melinda gave a startled cry, and jumped up on the table.

'That's it. I'm leaving,' she shrieked.

'Poor Deidre must be cold,' excused Jason. 'She just wants someone to cuddle her and warm her up.'

'Well, she's not cuddling me,' said Maureen bluntly.

'Ooh, I've always wanted to hold a snake,' said Christobel in an excited tone. 'Just to see if I *could*.'

Jason passed Deidre over, and Christobel shivered and squealed as Deidre hung off her arm and then slithered through her hair. Kirsty and I confined ourselves to touching her tail end. Wade also asked if he could hold her, while Frank and Melinda left in disgust.

'Your turn to bring your cat next week,' Jason said to me.

I said that I was sure that Tiger would much prefer lying by the fire at home to struggling to understand the Old Testament.

'Thank goodness for that!' said Liz.

WEEK·FOUR

Ancestors

Dave turned up this week. He apologized for missing last week's tutorial. He had strained a thigh muscle at soccer practice and had to rest his leg so that he could play on Saturday.

'At least you are here today, and without your canine friend,' said Liz in a not very sympathetic tone.

'Yes, but I'll have to whiz off in about 15 minutes to get to an appointment with my physiotherapist,' said Dave cheerfully.

Liz raised her eyebrows but made no comment other than to say that those of us who were here last week looked at Genesis 1–11, sometimes referred to as the "Primeval story". Today we were supposed to consider Genesis 12–50, sometimes called the "Patriarchal story".'

'Which is frightfully misogynistic, because women have just as important a role as men,' declared Christobel with a toss of her head. 'It's all very well to call Abraham "Father Abraham", but he wouldn't ever have become a father if it hadn't been for the women who bore his children.'

'What was that song we used to teach the kids at Sunday School?' Maureen thought aloud. 'Oh, yes, it went something like:

Father Abraham has many sons
Many sons has Father Abraham
And I am one of them
And so are you
So let's all praise the Lord ...

But no one sings:

Mother Sarah has many daughters
Many daughters has Mother Sarah
And I am one of them
And so are you
So let's all praise the Lord ... '

'You see, "sons" refers to everybody,' explained Dave, 'but "daughters" can only be women.'

'So I have to put up with being designated a "son", which suppresses my female identity, but you can't put up with being an honorary "daughter",' said Christobel with eyes flashing.

'Perhaps,' suggested Maureen, 'we could sing:

Parents Sarah and Abraham
Have many children
Many children have parents Sarah and Abraham
And I am one of them
And so are you
So let's all praise the Lord ... '

'But it doesn't really fit the music,' observed Kirsty.

'I think that Christobel has made an important point about the role of women in Genesis,' intervened Liz, 'and from now on perhaps it would be less sexist if we referred to chapters

12–50 as the "Ancestral story". So what kind of literature is it?'

'History,' said Frank belligerently. 'The *Patriarchal history* to be exact. The history of the patriarchs.'

'Legend,' retorted Wade. '*Foundation legends* to be exact. Legends about the founding mothers and fathers of the Israelite nation.'

Melinda glared at him.

'I won't bother to quote New Testament texts which show that Jesus and the first Christians accepted that Genesis 12–50 was historical because I know that you won't believe *them*. Perhaps you will be more impressed by the extensive archaeological evidence which has been uncovered which supports their historicity?'

'Yeah,' said Frank, 'how are you going to get around that?'

'Easily,' responded Wade coolly. 'Archaeologists may have found that some of the names and customs mentioned in Genesis actually existed in the second millennium BCE but, despite what is implied in conservative books on the Bible, they have not been able to *prove* that Sarah and Abraham, Leah, Rachel, Jacob, and so on, were real people. No one has been able to verify supposed historical events in Genesis with evidence outside the Bible. No Egyptian records have been found which show that a man called Joseph was Pharaoh someone-or-other's right-hand man in years so-and-so. No one has been able to establish beyond doubt the dates when the patriarchs and matriarchs would have lived. Archaeology is certainly fascinating, but findings so far have been far from conclusive!'

'I pity anyone who has so little faith that he can think that the Word of God contains *legends*,' exclaimed Melinda to the room in general.

'But are legends necessarily untrue?' asked Ruth. 'I mean,

we speak about sporting heroes and movie stars as "legends", people like Elvis Presley and Marilyn Monroe, but no one denies that they once existed.'

'They just deny that they're dead,' said Jason.

'I hardly think that Elvis and Marilyn belong in the same category as Abraham and Sarah,' snapped Melinda.

'I don't know,' pondered Christobel. 'Sarah was supposed to be frightfully beautiful, and she was regarded as a sex object and dreadfully exploited. When they went to Egypt, rotten old Abraham made her pretend to be his sister so that she could get placed in Pharaoh's harem and he'd get lots of sheep and donkeys!'

'Pig,' muttered Maureen. 'And that's only in chapter 12. The poor old thing had to go through the same thing again in chapter 20 with King Abilech or whatever he was called. And when I say poor old thing, I mean *old* thing. It says in chapter 17 that she was 90! I know that some old ladies can be quite nice-looking for their age, but surely it's stretching credibility too far to believe that the Abi-person would still desire her? She should have been in a nursing home, not a harem.'

'And, according to Genesis 26, Abimelech was king of the Philistines,' Wade pointed out, 'but the Philistines didn't colonize Canaan until about 1150 BCE, hundreds of years after the time when Abraham was supposed to have lived. It was after Moses' time, too, but the Elohist writing the story in the ninth century would have been familiar with them.'

'We are not going to engage in that silly exercise of dividing Genesis 12–50 into J, E, and P?' asked Melinda curtly. 'Such source divisions are highly debatable … '

'Highly demonic, I'd say,' said Frank.

'And as far as the Philistines are concerned,' continued Melinda, 'although the main colonization may not have taken place until after 1150 BC, there must have been small groups who settled there in the patriarchal period.'

Frank nodded and Wade gave a scornful laugh.

'Can we just clarify what type of literature we are dealing with?' interjected Liz.

'Genesis 12–50 doesn't seem to be a straightforward historical report,' answered Ruth, considering the matter, 'and it isn't like a modern biography. I wonder whether you could describe it as a collection of cherished stories or traditions that have been passed on by the tribes of Israel from one generation to the other? I don't think that the Yahwist, Elohist, and priestly writer invented them, but they may have been responsible for putting them into writing.'

'And you can't expect oral traditions to be handed down for hundreds of years without being altered or added to in some way,' remarked Wade. 'In particular, it would have been easy for different versions of stories to come about. That was probably what happened with the story of the matriarchal ancestor being passed off as a sister and placed in a foreign ruler's harem. Genesis 12:10–20; 20:1–18; and 26:1–11 are doubtless different versions of the one story.'

'There is no reason why they could not have been separate incidents,' maintained Melinda. 'Despite some similarities there are clear differences in detail.'

Frank agreed.

'You won't give in, will you?' sighed Wade.

'Why do we have to get so hung up on whether the stories really happened or not?' Christobel burst out. 'We should remember that story-telling was frightfully important in ancient cultures. We still tell children bedtime stories, of course, but sadly lots of adults despise fiction as "untrue" and want to read things that are factual, like newspapers (only, of course, what most newspapers report aren't facts at all, but only journalists' interpretations of what happened). But, be that as it may, story-telling is an absolutely vitally important way of conveying meaning and values and forming a child's identity. When my nieces and nephew come to stay with me I utterly refuse to read them any books which contain violence or are demeaning to women. They'll never hear from me a story about Father Rabbit going off to work on the farm while Mother Rabbit cleans the house and bakes carrot cake. I spend simply ages in bookshops looking for children's stories in which the female characters are strong, independent role models ... '

'I can see what you mean,' said Maureen, 'and I'm all for Mother Rabbit roaring around the paddock on the tractor while Father Rabbit hangs out the washing and does the ironing. If there's one thing I hate it's washing and ironing, and I don't know why but I've always had a sneaking desire to drive a tractor. However, I think that "political correctness" sometimes goes a bit too far with kids' books. I've been a *Thomas the Tank Engine* fan ever since I baby-sat the neighbour's little girl a few years ago and we watched her *Thomas* video. Really nice it was, narrated by Ringo Starr and all. But wasn't there a fuss in the papers about it being sexist?'

'The thing is, all the main characters, the strong steam engines, are male,' said Christobel. 'The female characters, Annie and Clarabell, are just carriages who giggle and chat while they are pulled along by Thomas.'

'There's Daisy the Diesel Engine,' contributed Kirsty.

'Isn't that the one with the long eyelashes and the seductive voice?,' asked Christobel. 'Another appalling stereotype!'

'Well, we all know what happened to steam engines,' said Maureen with a laugh. 'It's Daisy's daughters who now dominate the railway yards!'

'Oh, good grief, is that the time? I must be off,' said Dave, and he rushed toward the door, then, remembering his ailment, hobbled out of view.

'Can we get back to the point?' asked Wade impatiently.

'What is the point? That the ancestral stories are full of good, inspiring role models for future generations of Israelites to follow?' pursued Maureen. 'I must say, I actually thought that the ancestors were a pretty motley lot. All they did was lie, cheat, quarrel, and have sex. And speaking of sex, I thought that it was pretty off the way husbands could have more than one wife, and one of Abraham's excuses for letting Pharaoh or the Abi-person think that Sarah was his sister was that she really *was* his half-sister. They had the same father. If that's not incestuous, what is? I suppose that everyone has a few skeletons in the family closet, but no sensible person parades them about as though they were actually proud of them, so why did the Israelites?'

'And, ironically, Jacob, the one who ended up being called Israel, was just about the worst of the lot,' added Christobel.

'That's right,' agreed Maureen. 'It was downright awful the way he treated his poor older brother, although his father was a silly old fool to be tricked into giving the wrong son his blessing.'

'But doesn't it strike you as significant that younger sons nearly always end up on top in the ancestral narratives,' asked Wade, 'in view of the fact that David and Solomon were also younger sons? The Jahwist, their national historian, was doubtless promoting the "younger sons" theme to support their claims to power.'

'Abraham is a very inspiring role model when it comes to faith, obedience, and trust in God,' proclaimed Melinda forcefully.

Frank agreed.

'Actually, I thought that he was a bit of a wimp,' replied

Maureen. 'He did whatever Sarah told him too, like when she said that he should sleep with her slave Hagar so that Hagar could have a child for her. Then, when Sarah had a child of her own, and didn't want Hagar's any more, she made Abraham send poor Hagar and the kid away, even though he didn't want to. And incidentally, that reminds me, how come Hagar left carrying the child on her shoulder, when it says a couple of chapters earlier that he was 13 years old? There's no way that I could have carried my son Neil when he was 13 even if I'd wanted to, but I'm sure that I would have thought that the lazy little so-and-so had legs of his own and could walk by himself … '

'Maureen, I'm afraid that you've misread the text,' said Melinda. 'It only says that Abraham put water and food on Hagar's shoulder.'

'What version have you got?' demanded Maureen. 'Oh, the NIV. Well, it distinctly says in my NRSV: "Abraham rose early in the morning, and took bread and a skin of water, and gave it to Hagar, putting it on her shoulder, *along with the child* … "'

'That means that he gave the child bread and water, too,' said Frank.

'It is a difficult verse to translate,' conceded Liz, 'but the context seems to suggest that a very young child is being referred to.'

'I knew I was right,' said Maureen with satisfaction.

'It is only a minor detail, anyway,' continued Melinda dismissively. 'What is important is that one of the great themes of Genesis is faith and obedience, and Abraham's supreme test of faith and obedience came when God told him to sacrifice his beloved son Isaac. He nobly went ahead and would have done it if God hadn't intervened at the last moment and provided a ram.'

'Yeah, Abraham is a model of the Father "who did not spare his own son, but gave him up for us all" (Romans 8:32), and Isaac is a model of Christ "obedient to death" (Philippians 2:5–8),' said Frank with a pleased expression.

'Isaac didn't have any say in it at all!' screamed Christobel. 'It is an appalling story! And it is so vividly written – the author manages to convey such tension, such pathos! I can just see father and son walking up the hill, little Isaac trying valiantly to carry the firewood. Then he says, so trustingly, so innocently, "Daddy, here is the firewood, but where is the lamb for the burnt offering?" It upsets me every time I read it.'

'The story clearly reflects the transition from child sacrifice to animal sacrifice in ancient society,' concluded Wade.

'You would say that,' said Melinda grimly.

'Isn't it also part of one of the main themes or motifs of the ancestral story,' put in Ruth, 'the threat to the promise?'

Liz asked Ruth to explain.

'On one hand, every so often throughout the Abraham and Sarah stories there is mention of God's promises. Chapter 12 starts off with God promising Abraham that he will make of him a great nation, make his name great, and make him a blessing to all the families of the earth. Then God promises in chapter 13 that he will give Abraham and his offspring the land of Canaan, and that his offspring will be as numerous as the dust of the earth. In chapter 15 it is that the offspring will be as numerous as the stars in the sky.'

'What that means is that Abraham's earthly children, the Jews, will be like dust, while his spiritual children, Christians, will be like stars,' interrupted Frank.

'That isn't what the text says,' responded Liz abruptly.

'No, it's absolutely frightful theology!' exclaimed Christobel. 'The sort of thinking that has contributed to anti-Semitism throughout the centuries.'

'I thought that the references to dust and stars just signified that Abraham would have so many descendants that they would be impossible to count,' went on Ruth quietly, 'which was an amazing thing to promise a man whose wife was quite advanced in years and had been unable to have any children. And Abraham and Sarah had to wait years and years for the promise to be partially fulfilled with the birth of Isaac. While they were waiting they tried various ways to fulfil the promise in their own way, such as by adopting a nephew as their heir and then getting Hagar, the poor slave girl, pregnant. Also they faced a number of threats to the promise, such as when Sarah twice ended up in a foreign ruler's harem. That raised the awful prospect that if she did conceive, Abraham would not be the father! But I suppose that the ultimate threat to the promise came when Abraham almost sacrificed Isaac.'

'It's a bit like a soap opera, isn't it?' commented Maureen.

Melinda gasped in disbelief.

'The Word of God is not a *soap opera*!'

'How about narrative?' asked Liz. 'Claus Westermann, in his commentary on Genesis 12–50, says that "a narrative portrays an event as it moves through climax to resolution".'

'So if I was to approach one or more of these chapters from a literary perspective for my essay, I would concentrate on working out the plot, the setting, the catalyst that gets the action going, the complication or complications that arise, and the resolution,' said Ruth.

'Yes,' said Liz, 'and you could try to discern key themes and images, the writer's style, use of irony, and so forth. The literary approach works really well with Genesis 12–50 because there are so many good stories in it that really are literary works of art.'

'And if I was to approach it from a historical perspective, I'd have to try to sort out who wrote it and when it was likely to have been written, and whether the sacrifice of Isaac was linked to child sacrifice in ancient society, and all that sort of thing,' remarked Maureen.

'Exactly,' agreed Liz.

'Well, I think I'll stick to literary,' said Maureen. 'The other seems too hard.'

'What really interests me is the ideology behind the text,' declared Wade. 'As Ruth said a while ago, throughout chapters 12–17 God promises Abraham that he will give him and his descendants the land of Canaan. But he enters Canaan as an immigrant, not an invader and conqueror. The Book of Joshua is full of bloody stories of conquest and extermination of the Canaanites, but Genesis shows that Abraham respected the rights of the indigenous inhabitants of Canaan, entered into treaties with them, went to their aid when they were attacked by enemies, shared hospitality with them, joined in the worship of their gods, *bought* land for Sarah's burial plot … '

'Worshipped their gods!' cried Melinda. 'He most certainly did not!'

'Read chapter 14,' retorted Wade. 'After rescuing the people and goods of the king of Sodom, Abraham met King Melchizedek of Salem, a priest of "El Elyon" (the chief Canaanite deity). The priest/king blessed him, and Abraham gave him a tenth of his booty.'

'Melchizedek's understanding of God was doubtless imperfect,' contended Melinda, 'but Abraham bore testimony to the one true God by telling him and the king of Sodom that he had sworn by the "Lord [Yahweh], God Most High, creator of heaven and earth", that he would not accept any of the king of Sodom's property.'

'And quite right, too, considering the wickedness of the Sodomites,' said Frank.

'But Abraham was not anti-Sodom. Apart from helping the Sodomites in battle, he interceded for them in chapter 18,' argued Wade. 'I hope that you are not going to launch into one of those of tired old tirades against homosexuality, because chapters 18 and 19 do not actually say that the sin of Sodom which provoked God's wrath was homosexuality. What was so abhorrent about the attempted attack on Lot's angelic visitors was the fact that it was going to be *violent gang rape*. That is surely not grounds for condemning acts of love between two consenting adults!'

'1 Corinthians 6 … ' began Frank ominously.

'Oh, we are not here to discuss Corinthians,' snapped Christobel. 'What I find so abhorrent about the Sodom story is that rotten old Lot offered the rapists his two virgin daughters as substitutes for the male guests. Typical of ancient (and tragically not so ancient) attitudes to women! But what struck me when you were talking just now, Wade, was that although the Canaanites get a frightfully bad press in the rest of the Bible, Tamar was a Canaanite, and she became the ancestor of David!'

'Is she the one who dressed up as a prostitute and tricked her father-in-law into having sex with her?' asked Maureen. 'Another odd story, I thought.'

'She was in an absolutely dreadful situation,' explained Christobel. 'A childless widow was practically a social outcast. She no longer belonged in her father's household, yet she had no real ties with her husband's clan, and no children to support and protect her in her old age. Partly to help overcome this, the Israelites came up with the idea that a brother of a dead male should marry his widow and father children for him, thus carrying on his name.'

'Which means that it was ultimately for the benefit of the dead man, not his poor widow,' pointed out Maureen. 'I sure am glad that custom died out. My ex-brother-in-law is a pain in the neck. It would have been worse marrying him than Don, if Don had died, which he didn't, unfortunately.'

'Of course, it was a frightful patriarchal society,' went on Christobel, 'and much as I hate to admit it, women did *need* husbands and children. But Tamar's husband's brother didn't want to do his duty. He still went ahead and had his pleasure, forcing himself on poor Tamar, but he withdrew in time to spill his semen on the ground so that she couldn't get pregnant. Then he died (good riddance), and his father, rotten old Judah, refused to let his youngest son marry Tamar. So she came up with a simply brilliant plan for outwitting him and getting pregnant. She disguised herself and tricked him into thinking that she was a prostitute. He couldn't resist having sex with her, and then she took his signet, cord, and staff. Some time later, when he found out that his daughter-in-law had become pregnant, he was furious and ordered that she be burnt to death. (Note that it was OK for men to sleep with prostitutes, it was a different story when women indulged in non-marital sex!) Then Tamar triumphantly produced Judah's signet, cord, and staff and said, "It was the owner of these who made me pregnant." He was left looking a fool, and she gave birth to twins, one of whom is supposed to have been King David's ancestor.'

'As I said earlier, there are certainly some well-composed stories in Genesis, and this is one of them,' said Liz.

'I liked the story of Isaac and Rebekah,' confided Kirsty. 'It was so nice and romantic the way Isaac fell in love with her as soon as he saw her, and she comforted him after his mother's death.'

'That's all very well, but it was Rebekah's father and brother who decided that she would marry Isaac,' said Maureen. 'She didn't have any say in it at all. She was just expected to go off with a complete stranger at the drop of a hat, and probably never see her family again. Her poor mother wanted to keep her with her for at least 10 days, but off she had to go. It would have broken my heart if I'd been her mother, but a woman's feelings apparently didn't count back then.'

'Rebekah was happy to go because she knew that it was God's will,' observed Melinda.

'Oh, it was no doubt very exciting for her going off like that,' replied Maureen, 'young people can be so irresponsible. It's her mother I feel sorry for. And even if Isaac did end up falling in love with her, she couldn't have a baby at first, and then she had two horrible twins, and when they grew up they provided her with horrible daughters-in-law, so it's not a nice story at all.'

'I've never really liked the Rachel/Leah story, either,' admitted Ruth. 'It is such a sad portrayal of rivalry and bitterness between sisters.'

'It certainly underlines the importance of having children,' said Christobel. 'To be infertile must have been an absolutely terrible thing.'

'But Jacob loved Rachel even though she didn't have any children at first,' Kirsty pointed out.

'And Leah had her children as consolation for Jacob not loving her,' remarked Maureen. 'I know just how she must have felt. It hurts like hell when you are rejected, but you make the best of what you've got and concentrate on your kids.'

'Time is running away,' intervened Liz, 'and we haven't got onto the Joseph story yet. What did you make of that?'

'I was really shocked,' said Maureen. 'His father didn't give him a coat of many colours at all. It says in my NRSV that it was just a long robe with sleeves. So much for all those years

I got the kids at Sunday School to get out their crayons and colour away!'

'The point of the story is that it was clearly a luxurious gift which made his brothers jealous,' commented Wade.

'And I don't blame them,' Maureen went on. 'Joseph must have been a right precocious pain in the neck.'

'He was certainly naïve and foolish to tell his brothers about his dream of them bowing down to him,' said Ruth.

'But his prophecy was eventually fulfilled,' declared Melinda. 'Although they mistreated him terribly by selling him to slave traders on their way to Egypt, God was in control and it all worked out for the best. Joseph's story is a very inspiring testimony to the way that God can bring great good out of seeming misfortunes.'

'So that's its purpose, is it?' asked Maureen.

'No, it is simply a literary device to get the Israelites to Egypt so that the Exodus can take place in the next book,' said Wade provocatively.

Kirsty, who had been trying earnestly to follow the discussion, looked almost ready to burst into tears.

'I'm sorry, but I just can't help it. I've always thought that stories in the Bible were true, and if they're not, what about everything else that I've always believed about Jesus and God and everything? It's like the rug is getting ripped out from under my feet and I don't know what I should believe any more.'

'Claus Westermann, whom I mentioned earlier, argues that although Genesis was written in the first millennium, chapters 12–36 do reflect the life style of the second millennium, and so it is not impossible that some of the stories came from then,' responded Liz, trying to sound reassuring.

'I suspect that Christobel was on the right track when she reminded us of the way that stories help form a child's identity,' murmured Ruth. 'The same thing must be true of sporting clubs and army regiments, and such like. Stories (often based on fact) get passed on for years … '

'Yes, people sit around the bar raving on and on and if you're not a member of the club you get bored stiff,' said Maureen heatedly. 'When Don was secretary of the Golf Club … '

'I can accept that the Ancestral history helped to form the Israelites' identity,' interrupted Melinda. 'But another question we must address is what relevance does it have for us today?'

'Frankly, I haven't a clue,' said Maureen.

'What fascinates me is that the basic elements in human life haven't really changed over thousands of years,' remarked Ruth thoughtfully. 'I mean things like relationships and work. The struggle to make a living. Parents. Brothers. Sisters. Sibling rivalry. Love. Grief. The trauma of infertility. And underlying everything, God. I thoroughly agree with you, Melinda, that the Joseph story *is* an inspiring testimony to the way that God can bring good out of evil. And that is true of all the ancestral stories. No matter what their failings were, the ancestors were never abandoned by God. It is quite amazing the way God put up with them, and I don't know about you, but I find that very comforting! It reminds me of the hymn we sang at Mass this morning:

I will be Yahweh who walks with you!
You will be always within my hand!
Take your heart and give it all to Me!
Strong and constant is My love!
Strong and constant is My love!

'That could almost be the ancestors' theme song.'

Kirsty, looking a bit happier, agreed that this was reassuring, and I managed to say that I also found the ordinariness of the ancestors quite appealing. They certainly weren't saints, but then again, I had to admit that I wasn't either!

WEEK·FIVE

Exodus

I couldn't get to the Old Testament class yesterday. Toothache finally got the better of me and I had an 'emergency' appointment at the dentist's surgery. The only time available was right in the middle of the tutorial. Christobel and Maureen called around this evening to fill me in on what I'd missed. Maureen kindly brought some melt-in-the-mouth chocolate fudge cake. Apparently she always made it for her kids as a reward for being good when they went to the dentist. I privately thought it would have contributed to more visits to the dentist, but it was very nice.

When Maureen had finished telling me about her daughter Gail having bands on her teeth and her son Neil's abscess when he was eleven, I asked how things went yesterday.

'As usual, Melinda couldn't keep her mouth shut,' replied Christobel peevishly. 'She went on and on about how wonderful God was to raise up Moses to lead the Israelites out of Egypt, and how Moses was the most outstanding man in the Old Testament. Well, he might have been. There wasn't much competition. But what Melinda failed to point out was that Moses wouldn't have got anywhere if it hadn't been for the women in his life. First, there were the two midwives, Shiphrah and Puah, who were frightfully brave and defied Pharaoh's decree to kill all Israelite male infants at birth.

Then, when Pharaoh ordered that all male infants be chucked into the Nile, Moses' poor mother desperately tried to save him by putting him in a papyrus basket, sealed with bitumen. Then Pharaoh's daughter came along and rescued the baby from the river and nobly decided to keep him, and Moses' sister approached her and cleverly suggested that her mother could become the baby's nurse ...'

'You sure reminded everyone about them,' contributed Maureen.

'But do you know what Melinda said then?' cried Christobel. '"Yes, it is wonderful how God made sure that he was saved." God didn't have anything to do with it! Not directly, anyway! It is an absolutely wonderful account of how five women (four of them poor and oppressed, the lowest of the low in the society of the day) could take the initiative and outwit a horrible, nasty, seemingly all-powerful ruler.'

'What was it Wade said about the story of Moses' birth, Christobel?'

'That it is obviously a resistance legend set in the context of a hero legend. Of course, Frank had an absolute fit at the thought that anything in the Bible could be a *legend*, and Melinda said, with one of her supercilious smiles, "As Moses is the most important human being in the Old Testament, I hardly think that he could have been fictional."'

'But Wade had an answer for that too,' continued Maureen. 'He's never at a loss for words! He admitted that a historical person might lie behind all the traditions about Moses, but his story is so overlaid with legendary additions that it is impossible for us to get back to the "real" Moses.'

'And then, Michael,' Christobel rushed on, 'Frank went and said that as Moses actually wrote Exodus, he must have known what really happened! That started another one of those frightfully tedious debates about who actually wrote the

Pentateuch. Liz tried to say that, like Genesis, Exodus contains various traditions dating from different periods, but Melinda maintained that while there might have been some minor editing in later periods (under the inspiration of the Holy Spirit, of course), no modern scholarship that she has come across has convinced her that Moses could not have been the basic author.'

'I don't remember her saying that,' mused Maureen, 'but that might have been when I suddenly remembered that it is this Saturday that my cousin Dorothy and her husband Bruce are coming to dinner, and I was wondering whether I should make a curry or a roast.'

'Do your curry,' said Christobel firmly. 'The one you made for me was delicious.'

'Well, I think I will, because all you need is rice to go with it. You don't have to fuss around with vegetables, and I can never get roast potatoes to cook right. They either come out of the oven looking anaemic or burnt to a crisp. I expect Melinda can serve up perfect roast dinners,' Maureen added morosely, 'she's that sort of person.'

'Yes,' agreed Christobel, 'it's utterly sickening. What really annoys me is that it's hopeless trying to argue with her, because she's always so sure that she's right. So even though it was frightfully difficult, I kept quiet, but Ruth was brave enough to admit that she was rather attracted to the theory that Exodus was put together, in its final form at least, when the Israelites were in exile in Babylon in the sixth century BCE. They were once again in need of deliverance, so I suppose the story of the Exodus would have been awfully encouraging for them.'

'Oh, yes, I do remember *that*,' said Maureen proudly, 'because I said: "But did it really happen?" And Wade replied, "An exodus of a million plus Israelites is beyond belief, but it is not unlikely that *some* Israelites were slaves in Egypt and managed to escape." That made Melinda say (quite sarcastically), "I am relieved to know that you at least acknowledge that an exodus *might* have happened. I had begun to think that you were incapable of believing anything at all."'

'Yes, and then we got into that terribly tedious argument about *when* it might have happened,' sighed Christobel. 'Frank maintained that it would have been in 1446 or 1445 BCE, because it says in 1 Kings 6:1 that the Exodus happened 480 years before the founding of the temple in the fourth year of King Solomon's reign, which would have been in about 967/66. But Wade insisted that it couldn't have been in the fifteenth century because archaeologists have shown that the cities that Exodus 1:11 says the Israelites built in Egypt didn't exist until the thirteenth century, and therefore most serious scholars accept a thirteenth-century date for the Exodus.'

'But Melinda stuck to the fifteenth-century date, and she and Wade got into an argument about who could produce the better archaeological evidence,' said Maureen rolling her eyes. 'So I said, "How about we compromise and settle for a fourteenth-century date?", but no one seemed to think that was a very good idea.'

'I thought it was an excellent suggestion,' affirmed Christobel loyally, 'but the thing is, there's absolutely no historical proof whatsoever that the events described in Exodus actually happened, so Liz, who was looking rather tired by this time, asked if we could leave the historical debates behind and just consider the text as literature. That prompted Ruth to say that it was a good story, and I think she also said something about the irony of Moses being rescued by Pharaoh's daughter and brought up in Pharaoh's court, because he was the one God had chosen to lead the Israelites out of Egypt.'

'And then Kirsty said that it was nice the way Moses' mother got to look after him,' recalled Maureen. 'I suppose it was better than seeing him die, but personally I don't know how I could have put up with pretending that another woman was my child's mother, and I was just the nanny who had to take orders.'

'Then,' said Christobel with a giggle, 'Wade was frightfully naughty and declared that a remarkable birth was typical of a hero legend, and that long before Exodus was written a similar story was told in the ancient Near East about Sargon, mighty king of Agade, whose mother also hid him in a basket of rushes, sealed with bitumen, and put him in a river. I'm sure that he only said it to stir Melinda and Frank up. You should have seen the look Melinda gave him. I thought Frank was going to explode!'

'Wasn't it after that that Jason reckoned that Moses didn't come across as much of a hero to him?' asked Maureen. 'It wasn't so much heroic as impetuous the way he lost his temper and killed an Egyptian who was beating up an Israelite, and then he ran from Egypt and hid from Pharaoh at the back of beyond, working as a shepherd for years and years until he stumbled across a burning bush which talked.'

'But it wasn't the bush that talked,' gurgled Christobel. 'That's what Jason said, but Melinda quickly corrected him: it says in 3:2 that "the angel of the Lord appeared to him in a flame of fire".'

'But later on it seems that it is God, not an angel, talking,' objected Maureen. 'Very confusing.'

'So Frank explained that an angel got Moses' attention, then God spoke to him,' revealed Christobel, 'which made Jason flippantly remark that the angel must have been God's private secretary.'

'I suppose that the Lord of the universe is entitled to a

private secretary,' said Maureen fairly, flicking through her Bible. 'When he did speak, he said … oh yes, here it is, in chapter 3:

> I have observed the misery of my people who are in Egypt: I have heard their cry on account of their taskmasters. Indeed, I know their sufferings, and I have come down to deliver them from the Egyptians, and to bring them up out of that land to a good and broad land, a land flowing with milk and honey, to the country of the Canaanites, the Hittites, the Amorites, the Perizzites, the Hivites, and the Jebusites.

'As Jason said, great news for the Israelites, not so good for the Canaanites, Hittites, Amorites, Perizzites, Hivites, and Jebusites! But before Moses could get too excited, God dropped another bombshell: Moses was the one he'd chosen to lead the Israelites out of Egypt. Poor old Moses nearly had a fit. "Not me! You can't be serious! They'll never listen to me! I couldn't possibly!" Well, that's not exactly what he said, but it's close enough.'

'Melinda's response to that was that Moses was naturally conscious of being an unworthy sinner,' interjected Christobel, 'but Wade declared that whoever wrote chapter 3 was clearly following a stereotype of a prophetic call. True prophets in the Old Testament invariably show reluctance.'

'And who could blame them?' commented Maureen. 'By the looks of things they couldn't expect an easy life, to say the least. And I really don't think that God did much to reassure Moses. When Moses wanted to know whom he should tell the Israelites the God of their ancestors was (they appear to have forgotten all about him), God just said, "Say to the Israelites, 'I AM has sent me to you.'" What sort of an answer is that? The Israelites would have thought he was nuts.'

'But then God is supposed to have revealed that his name was Yahweh,' said Christobel, 'so of course we had to discuss that. Liz told us that it seems to be from the Hebrew verb "to be" which some scholars think means "he will be", "he is", or "he who causes things to be", but I think *she* who causes things to be is the best possible translation. Mother God, the source of all being ...'

'I thought things were going to get real nasty there, Michael,' continued Maureen with a laugh, 'Frank went on about there being nothing in Exodus which says that God is a woman, and Christobel lost her temper and said that that was because Exodus was written by men. But Ruth intervened in that quiet way she's got (I wish I had it too) and said something about who God is, and how he/she can be named being still a controversial subject, but perhaps that is because God is ultimately beyond our comprehension and no simple answer can be given. However, God did give Moses the assurance that "I will be with you," which I suppose was quite nice.'

'Jason was more impressed by his "groovy staff" which he could turn into a snake,' remembered Christobel.

'Yes, well, he would be, liking snakes the way he does. Can't think of anything worse, myself, than having a snake as a pet. When my kids were little I put up with frogs and stick insects and goodness knows what else they took a fancy to, but I would have put my foot down if they'd wanted a snake. And anyway, a snake-staff might have impressed the Israelites, but it didn't work on Pharaoh. His wise men and sorcerers could turn their staffs into snakes too. Frank said that showed the power of the Devil, and the way he tries to counterfeit God's miracles. But I must admit, I found the competition between Moses and the Egyptian sorcerers to make snakes and see who could set off the worst plagues a bit far-fetched.'

'Wade's explanation for the plagues was that gnats, locusts, and frogs, and so on were natural phenomena in Egypt,' said Christobel. 'So what could have happened was that the Egyptians suffered from a series of natural disasters. The Israelite slaves took advantage of their mistresses' and masters' misfortunes and fled to the border, and once successfully out of Egypt they interpreted the disasters as the work of their god. I thought that was quite plausible, but Melinda insisted that while God might have used natural phenomena, the plagues were still supernatural in origin, because they were accurately predicted ahead of time, and the Israelites were spared.'

'Then Frank went on about it being a contest between the one true God and the false gods of Egypt, represented by Pharaoh, who probably thought he was a god,' added Maureen. '"God sure did punish him. It doesn't pay to go against God," etc., etc. However, Kirsty (who as usual was having a bit of trouble keeping up, poor dear) asked why God kept hardening Pharaoh's heart so that he wouldn't release the Israelites? Good question, I thought. I'd been wondering the same thing myself. According to Melinda, it was because God is ultimately in control of all things and so Pharaoh was not really free to oppose him, but his continued resistance gave God opportunities to display his power and might. Well, God might have enjoyed sitting up in heaven creating frogs and watching them crawl all over Pharaoh's bed. I had a bit of a laugh at that myself. But I think that he could have found better ways of showing off than killing every living first-born creature in Egypt, animal and human. Downright over-the-top and nasty, I call that.'

Christobel absolutely agreed. 'Melinda then insisted that the Egyptians deserved punishment for the way that they had treated the Israelites, and God protected the Israelites by instructing Moses and his brother Aaron to tell the Israelites to sacrifice a poor little lamb and put its blood on their door posts so that he would "pass over" their houses and not destroy their first-born. And hence the Israelites came to celebrate the religious festival known as the Passover to commemorate the exodus, and eat unleavened bread to remind them of the haste with which they left Egypt. Well, you'll never guess, Michael, what Wade said then.'

I couldn't.

'That the Passover was originally a nomadic shepherd's festival! Before shepherds departed in spring for summer pastures, they would sacrifice an animal and put blood on their tent posts in a ceremony to ward off evil spirits. After the Israelites left Egypt, they adopted this custom to commemorate the Exodus, and combined it with a feast of unleavened bread, originally a Canaanite spring barley harvest ceremony. Frank was frightfully cross, but Ruth said that what fascinated her was that the instructions for the leaving of Egypt and the Passover in chapter 12 are actually *instructions for liturgy*. "This day shall be a day of remembrance for you. You shall celebrate it as a festival to the Lord; throughout your generations you shall observe it as a perpetual ordinance," etc. It was through the liturgy of the Passover that future generations of Israelites were able to share in God's once-and-for-all saving act, made present for them, just as Christians experience a re-presentation or rendering present of Christ's unique sacrifice on the Cross in the liturgy of the Eucharist (at least in the Catholic tradition). I'd never thought of it like that before.'

'How did Frank react to that?' I managed to say.

'Oh, he was frightfully un-ecumenical and said that he didn't go along with "all that rubbish" about a Catholic priest being able to create Christ's real body and blood,' replied

Christobel, 'but he did admit that Christ is our Passover lamb. It says so in 1 Corinthians 5:7. He saves us from sin and death. Hallelujah!'

'When we got onto the actual escape from Egypt, Jason reckoned that it was a bit like an ancient Western,' laughed Maureen. 'The goodies versus the baddies, and all that. And just when you think that the Israelites have got away safely, Yahweh hardens Pharaoh's heart again and makes him pursue them with his army.'

'Which Melinda again said was to show "his" power and glory,' muttered Christobel. 'Whoever wrote it might have thought that, but I think it is appallingly inaccurate to portray the divine mother, source of all being, as a violent warrior god on a quest for glory!'

'Yes, well, Melinda kept saying that the Egyptians were evil and idolatrous and deserved to be punished,' went on Maureen, 'and how wonderful it is that God intervenes to save those who trust in him, and how Moses stressed that it was all God's work. The people did nothing. As he told them in 14:13–14,

> Do not be afraid, stand firm, and see the deliverance that the Lord will accomplish for you today: for the Egyptians whom you see today you shall never see again. The Lord will fight for you, and you have only to keep still.'

'Which, according to Melinda, is supposed to contain a moral for today,' snapped Christobel. 'I suppose she meant that we should just pray, trust God, and do nothing. Sometimes that might be appropriate, but what good will it do if I pray to God to help the starving in the world, and don't lift a finger to help them myself?'

'Not much. And more often than not God doesn't answer

my prayers anyway,' admitted Maureen gloomily, 'but perhaps I expect too much. Instead of God waving a magic wand and getting me through the menopause in 60 seconds, I have to go and see doctors about hormone replacement therapy.'

'I am sure that God can work through doctors,' said Christobel firmly.

'Yes, but I could do with some guidance at the moment on which doctor I should go along to. I want someone who'll … you know … be understanding. I don't think my current GP thinks of his patients as people: just Mr Ulcer, Miss Varicose Veins, Mrs Menopause, etc. You tell him your symptoms and his computer-like brain churns out a textbook response. Fed up with him, I asked to be referred to a gynaecologist. It cost the earth, and was a waste of money. I couldn't help but feel that he was more interested in delivering babies than helping women my age. The only thing he could suggest was that I wear a patch, but every time I put it on I get a terrible rash …'

'You need a female doctor,' exclaimed Christobel. 'I'll take you along to mine. She's frightfully understanding, and interested in the *whole* person. She's always running late because she spends simply ages listening to people, and she's open to alternative medicine. She recommended that I take Evening Primrose Oil tablets for PMT …'

'Was there any discussion about the crossing of the Red Sea?' I quickly asked, not feeling quite up to a discussion on female health matters.

'Oh, yes, Kirsty brought that up,' said Christobel, reverting back to Exodus. 'She thought it must have been very exciting when Moses stretched out his hand and the waters parted. But Wade objected that it wasn't the *Red* Sea that the Israelites crossed, a more accurate translation of the Hebrew word is "*Reed* Sea". If it had been the Red Sea, it would have taken the Israelites more than a night to get over to the other side, and the east wind which blew the water away would have blown it right into their faces! It is more likely (said Wade) that the Israelites just crossed a small reedy marsh which had been dried by a strong wind, but then a violent rain storm followed, and the Egyptian chariots following behind got bogged down. Poor Kirsty looked awfully downcast at that. I don't mind Wade having a go at Melinda and Frank (it doesn't seem to make the slightest dent in their convictions anyway), but Kirsty seems so … so … vulnerable.'

'Mmm. What I didn't understand was how they got across the Red Sea, if it wasn't the Red Sea they crossed in chapter 14,' remarked Maureen, 'but I'd forgotten that the Suez Canal hadn't been built then, so I suppose they didn't have to cross water at all.'

'I thought that we were going to get as bogged down as the Egyptian chariots talking about it,' said Christobel, 'but Ruth got back to the literary focus instead of history focus, and pointed out that the writer of the story is mainly trying to make the point that it was God who saved the Israelites, however it happened, and then they believed in him and Moses, and led by Miriam and Moses sang songs of praise.'

'Well, they didn't stay grateful for long,' said Maureen. 'Scarcely any time passes before they're whinging about not having enough food and water, and wishing they were back in Egypt. I thought that was a bit off, but Jason said, "Hang on a minute, if you were wandering around a desert, wouldn't you be a bit worried about what was going on in the catering department? Especially if there didn't appear to be a catering department?" I had to admit that he had a point.'

'Frank then went on about it being a test,' said Christobel with a grimace, 'and while they failed dismally in their 40 years in the desert, Jesus, of course, succeeded in his 40 days in the wilderness. Someone (was it Ruth?) then pointed out that God did provide them with food, water, and protection from their enemies, but only one day at a time. They had to learn to trust him.'

'And it's not easy taking things one day at a time,' said Maureen with a sigh. 'I was lying awake last night thinking of all the bills that will be coming in the next few months, and wondering if I'll be able to afford a new dress for my niece Leanne's wedding, and whether I should make a cheesecake or an apple pie for dinner on Saturday, and whether I'd made an apple pie last time Dorothy and Bruce came to dinner or not, and how bad my memory is getting, and whether I'll get Alzheimer's when I'm old like Maud Scott, my old next-door neighbour, and it's all very well to say I'm trying to cross bridges before I come to them, but at night when you're on your own and you can't sleep you think of things like that ...'

'It's perfectly natural,' Christobel assured her.

'So did you eventually get Moses to Mount Sinai?' I asked, trying not to sound impatient.

'You mean the place where Moses had seen the burning bush and where the people made their covenant with God?' responded Maureen. 'Yes, and we had to talk about what exactly "covenant" means. Ruth said something about it referring to Israel's special relationship with God, while Wade reckoned that it was based on vassal treaties common in the ancient Near East. Apparently a king or lord would promise protection to a vassal or servant in return for loyalty and obedience. What happened next, Christobel?'

'I think that Ruth agreed that it might be similar to vassal treaties but it was based on God's love and care for the Israelites. As it says in 19:4–6,

You have seen what I did to the Egyptians, and how I bore you on eagles' wings and brought you to myself. Now therefore, if you obey my voice and keep my covenant, you shall be my treasured possession out of all the peoples. Indeed, the whole earth is mine, but you shall be for me a priestly kingdom and a holy nation.

'Wade was struck by what a remarkably egalitarian vision that is: everyone was to be equal! Power to the people, not to priests or kings! But sadly it was only a dream, never a reality in Israel's history.'

'No, they were a holy nation for about three minutes,' commented Maureen. 'As soon as the covenant was ratified with some horrible animal sacrifices and Moses went off up the mountain for another private chat with God, the people decided that they'd worship an image of a golden calf instead and throw a party, which Wade said probably meant an orgy, given the fertility associations of bull worship.'

'Melinda, of course, was frightfully disgusted at that,' said Christobel, 'but she talked about God graciously forgiving them and renewing the covenant. She *didn't* say, though, that according to chapter whatever it is "he" did lose his temper and tell Moses that he was going to destroy them. Fortunately Moses did some fast talking and got him to change his mind, but then Moses stormed down the mountain, destroyed the calf, and got the Levites to slay a few thousand Israelites, and God topped that punishment off with a plague to take care of a lot more,' Christobel finished with a shudder.

'Then Frank went on about Stephen in Acts 7, and the Jews forever opposing the Holy Spirit,' said Maureen. 'Just as they rejected Moses they rejected Christ. But Moses mediated with God on their behalf, just as Christ did on our behalf, or something or other. I think it was Ruth who then said that there never was a golden age of obedience in

Judaism or Christianity, we still sin and need reconciliation. I'm afraid I didn't pay much attention because I'd just remembered that I *had* made an apple pie the last time Dorothy and Bruce came for dinner, because it was American Independence Day and Bruce is into anything to do with America. I had to sit through four and a half hours of his slides of the Grand Canyon. The only thing that kept me awake was the indigestion caused by the apple pie. It was a nightmare, I can tell you!'

I said that it must have been, and did anything else happen in the tutorial?

'Oh, yes,' said Maureen, 'we had to look at those weird old laws. You know, what you should do if your ox falls down a pit or someone steals your sheep. "What's that got to do with religion?" I asked. Melinda reckoned it showed God's concern for all aspects of life, but Wade went on about the historical background to the laws: how they are similar to other ancient Near Eastern law codes, and must have originated in a settled agricultural community long after the Exodus. It was just claimed they were given by God at Mount Sinai to give them extra clout.'

'Actually, I think Wade was very impressed by their concern for the poor and oppressed,' disclosed Christobel, 'and I suppose there are some quite good ones: "You shall not wrong or oppress a resident alien, for you were aliens in the land of Egypt. You shall not abuse any widow or orphan … If you take your neighbour's cloak in pawn, you shall restore it before the sun goes down; for it may be your neighbour's only clothing to use as cover; in what else shall that person sleep?" etc., etc. But the frightful thing is women were still regarded as property. If a pregnant woman was hurt by someone and miscarried, compensation was to be paid to her husband!'

'Then there's that "eye for an eye, tooth for a tooth, hand

for a hand" law,' said Maureen, 'which I thought was pretty terrible too, although Liz said that it wasn't as bad as it looked. It was actually a law of limitation, designed to rule out uncontrolled revenge. You could *only* take an eye for an eye.'

'Which is still horrible,' declared Christobel. 'And not at all Christian. Jesus said in Matthew 5:38, "You have heard that it was said, 'An eye for an eye and a tooth for a tooth.' But I say to you, Do not resist an evildoer. But if anyone strikes you on the right cheek, turn the other also ..." '

'"So we don't have to worry about those old laws," I said to the group,' recalled Maureen, 'and Frank went on about us being saved by faith, not obeying the law. The Jews became slaves to the law, but it says in Romans that Christ has set us free, etc. That made Ruth say that she didn't think that law and grace were opposites in Exodus. God *graciously* gave the people the law so that they could build a decent society, and if we don't have to stick to the specific laws relating to ancient life, the Ten Commandments surely contain abiding ethical principles.'

'And Jesus didn't replace the Ten Commandments in the Sermon on the Mount,' Christobel pointed out, 'he took them further. For example: it isn't only wrong to commit murder, it is wrong to be angry with someone!'

'Now, I think that's going too far,' said Maureen. 'You'd have to be a saint not to get angry at times. But that wasn't what I was going to say. What was it? Oh, yes, after the Ten Commandments we got onto those laws about the Tabernacle: what the measurements should be, what the furniture should be, what priests should wear, and so on. About as interesting as Bruce's slide show, I thought, but Ruth said the tabernacle had to be got right because it was to be God's dwelling with the people. He was to travel with them after they left Mount Sinai, which I suppose was very nice of him, but the people couldn't just pop into the tabernacle for a chat whenever they felt like it. It was supposed to be too awesome and holy for that.'

'Wade said the instructions for the Tabernacle came from the priestly source,' contributed Christobel, 'and, being priests, they were frightfully into cultic things, horrible animal sacrifices, and so on, and they believed that God was so holy that a mortal couldn't see God and live.'

'Except Moses,' interjected Maureen.

'No, not even Moses. In the priestly account Moses only gets to see an amazingly awesome sort of fire cloud on the top of the mountain,' responded Christobel. 'Which is quite different from the Yahwist writer who talks about Moses going up the mountain with seventy elders of Israel, and they all see God, who seems much more human. He has a pavement of sapphire at his feet, and they eat and drink and have a good time.'

'That's in chapter 24, isn't it?' said Maureen. 'I got totally confused because Moses seemed to be leaping up and down the mountain like a flaming mountain goat. He must have been very fit, because he was quite old then.'

'According to Liz, a whole lot of different stories have been woven together,' explained Christobel. 'So you get the Yahwist account of Moses and the elders going up the mountain and "seeing" God in 24:9–11, and the totally different priestly account of Moses going into the fire cloud in 24:15–18. Likewise, Mount Sinai is sometimes called Mount Sinai and sometimes Horeb, and Moses' father-in-law is sometimes called Jethro and sometimes Reuel, which Liz said are further indications of different sources. Melinda would have liked to have disputed that, but we were running out of time, and Liz asked us a final question: What do we think is the significance of the book of Exodus? Ruth then said that it was foundational for Israel, because it contains the stories of the origins of the nation, the religious festival of the Passover and the feast of unleavened bread, the laws, and Israel's special relationship with God.'

'That's all very well for Jews, but what about us Christians?' inquired Maureen.

'Don't you remember? Wade said that the message of Exodus is still frightfully relevant for Christianity because it shows that God is a god of liberation who acts to rescue the poor and oppressed *in this world* (not just in heaven, like some Christians say), and liberation should involve the *whole* community. All too often Christians have privatized salvation, made it an individual thing, and God is concerned with *all* aspects of life, political, social, and economic as well as religious. Fortunately, liberation theologians are now recovering these insights into the way God works which are revealed in Exodus. In fact, the book of Exodus is of fundamental importance to liberation theology.'

'Oh, yes, I remember now,' said Maureen, 'because Melinda got het up because she thought liberation theologians were encouraging people to make revolutionary stands to overthrow unjust rulers, which is not what Exodus advocates because the Israelites did nothing. It was all God's work.'

'Well, I disagreed with her there,' said Christobel. 'God might have been given most of the credit for saving the Israelites, but humans had to act too. The midwives had to be frightfully brave and defy Pharaoh, and Moses had to stand up to him, and the people as a whole had to pack up and leave. Their treatment in Egypt might have been absolutely appalling, but it still would have taken courage to leave their birthplace and set off into the wilderness.'

'Pity their courage failed them later on,' concluded

Maureen. 'Frank thought there was a lesson in that for us, too. The Jews messed up their special relationship with God through lack of trust, but if we have faith and believe in the Lord Jesus Christ we will be saved. That prompted Ruth to say that what struck her about the Exodus, Mount Sinai stories, and the tabernacle instructions was the way early Christians borrowed their imagery and concepts to explain Christ. He is described in the New Testament as the lamb who was sacrificed to bring about our reconciliation with God, the high priest who intercedes for us ... I forget all the rest, but the writer of the Letter to the Hebrews goes on about it a lot.'

'I'm just glad we no longer have to sacrifice animals,' said Christobel. 'I think it would have been absolutely awful. Those dear little lambs. All that blood. Yuk!'

I agreed that I wouldn't have enjoyed it either.

'Yes, I'm a vegetarian in theory,' declared Maureen, 'but the trouble is, I can't resist a well-cooked steak or lamb chop. And, talking of steak, that reminds me, I must go shopping tomorrow and get all that I will need for dinner on Saturday. I wish that I'd never invited Dorothy and Bruce now, but they had me to a meal a few months ago, so I feel I have to return hospitality.'

Christobel sympathized with her.

'Anyway, Michael, that was about it,' she concluded. 'I don't think we've missed anything important, do you Maureen?'

Maureen shook her head.

'Was Dave there? You haven't mentioned him,' I asked.

'Oh, Dave, you'll never believe what he did!' exclaimed Christobel. 'I almost forgot. He arrived all right, but when he hunted in his sports bag for his Bible he discovered that his soccer socks were missing! Otto must have taken them out.

Dave said he's got a real thing about chewing socks. So Dave rushed off to buy some new ones. He said that his coach would kill him if he was late for the training session and didn't have the right gear!'

'Liz looked as if she'd like to kill him, too,' said Maureen, 'but he was gone before she could say anything.'

'I really do think that she could be a bit more assertive,' said Christobel. 'Not just with Dave. She lets Melinda talk far too much. Nobody else gets a chance.'

'Wade does,' corrected Maureen. 'That's another thing about Bruce. He talks non-stop, too, and Dorothy just sits there agreeing with everything he says. It's sickening. But I'm afraid we'd better go now, Christobel. I have to get home and start tidying up. What a strain entertaining is.'

I thanked them both for coming. In retrospect, a visit to the dentist didn't seem such a bad way of spending an hour after all.

WEEK·SIX

The Deuteronomic History

We got onto Deuteronomy today, the fifth and final Book of the Pentateuch. It's supposedly Moses' final teaching to the Israelites before he died and they crossed over into the land God had promised them. However, Liz said that in 1943 a German scholar called Martin Noth came up with the hypothesis that rather than being the last Book of the Pentateuch, Deuteronomy was actually the beginning of the 'Deuteronomic history', which includes the Books of Joshua, Judges, 1 & 2 Samuel and 1 & 2 Kings. These used to be referred to as 'the Former Prophets'. Prophecy does play an important role in them, but their language and theology betray such similarities to Deuteronomy that Noth concluded that, together with Deuteronomy, they form a Deuteronomic history put together during the sixth-century exile in Babylon.

'So on the surface Moses' speeches in Deuteronomy are addressed to the Israelites who were waiting to enter the Promised land in the thirteenth century,' said Ruth in an interested tone, 'but at a deeper level they may have been addressed to the Israelites who were hoping to return to the Promised land in the sixth century!'

'And they explain why the Israelites had been conquered and taken into exile,' asserted Wade. 'It wasn't because Yahweh was less powerful than the Babylonian gods, but because the Israelites had been unfaithful to him. "Moses" had given the people a choice: be faithful to Yahweh and obey his law and you will be blessed with peace and prosperity, be unfaithful and disobedient and you will be cursed with all kinds of disasters, culminating in military defeat. As it says in Deuteronomy 28:

> Because you did not serve the Lord your God joyfully and with gladness of heart for the abundance of everything, therefore you shall serve your enemies whom the Lord will send against you, in hunger and thirst, in nakedness and lack of everything. He will put an iron yoke on your neck until he has destroyed you. The Lord will bring a nation from far away, from the end of the earth, to swoop down on you like an eagle ... '

'Oh, don't read any more,' begged Christobel, 'there's all that frightful stuff about the people being besieged, and so starving that women would even eat their own children.'

'Which happened exactly as Moses said it would in the sixth century,' said Frank proudly. 'Jeremiah wrote about it in Lamentations: "The hands of compassionate women have boiled their own children ... "'

Christobel put her hands over her ears.

'Of course it happened exactly as "Moses" said,' exclaimed Wade, 'that's the whole point. The writer or editor of Deuteronomy knew it had happened and was explaining *why*.'

'Noth thought that the purpose of the Deuteronomic history was to justify the fall of the Israelite kingdoms of Israel in 722/1 and Judah in 587,' intervened Liz. 'No hope was given for the future, just an account of judgement. Do you agree that that is the case?'

'No, I don't,' answered Ruth, 'I think that there is hope for the future. After all, in 2 Samuel 7 God promises David that he will establish his kingdom forever, and 2 Kings ends with the last king of Judah being released from prison in Babylon. But, most of all, it says in Deuteronomy 30:

> When all these things have happened to you, the blessings and the curses that I have set before you, if you call them to mind among all the nations where the Lord your God has driven you, and return to the Lord your God, and you and your children obey him with all your heart and with all your soul, just as I am commanding you today, then the Lord your God will restore your fortunes and have compassion on you, gathering you again from all the peoples among whom the Lord your God has scattered you. Even if you are exiled to the ends of the world, from there the Lord your God will gather you, and from there will bring you back into the land that your ancestors possessed … '

'You'd think Noth would have had more to worry about in 1943 than when the Bible was written,' commented Maureen. 'But I can remember my main concern was food rations, and not getting any sweets until a kind American airman gave me a packet of chewing gum one day. But, of course, I was only a kid. Noth would have been much older. Perhaps he was upset by the war, and that made him so pessimistic.'

'I am afraid that his hypothesis is just one of many conflicting ones put forward by liberal scholars this century,' declared Melinda. 'But the Bible itself testifies that Moses produced a written book. I quote from Deuteronomy 31:24–26: "When Moses had finished writing down in a book the words of this law to the very end, Moses commanded the Levites who carried the ark of the covenant of the Lord [a box containing the stone tablets with the Ten Commandments written on them], saying, 'Take this book of the law and put it beside the ark of the covenant of the Lord your God'." That clearly refers to the book we know as Deuteronomy.'

'Then how did Moses manage to write about his own death in Deuteronomy 34?' asked Jason with a grin.

'He was guided by the Holy Spirit,' said Frank.

'That must have been a later addition,' conceded Melinda, 'but Moses would have written the bulk of the book.'

'Another widely-held theory is that an early edition of Deuteronomy was the "book of the law" which was found in the temple in the seventh century in the reign of King Josiah,' said Liz, 'and it formed the basis of his reform programme, described in 2 Kings 23. He suppressed pagan religious practices and insisted on the exclusive worship of Yahweh, which was centralized at the Jerusalem temple.'

'Yes, the Deuteronomic history could well have been originally composed as propaganda to justify his policies,' expounded Wade, 'and it was later edited and "brought up to date" in the exile. It would have been ironic, though, if that was the case. Josiah, the great king who follows the covenant and does all the right things, ends up not blessed with peace and prosperity but with death in battle!'

'Sadly, Josiah was almost exceptional in his devotion to the Lord,' explained Melinda, 'and his good reign only postponed the judgement that was inevitable, as it says in 2 Kings 22:15–20. His predecessor Manasseh was particularly wicked. He promoted disgusting pagan religious practices, astrology, magic, divination, even human sacrifice: he had his own son burned alive! Such wickedness was infectious, it not only affected the royal court but corrupted the people.'

'I found a lovely prayer of Manasseh,' contributed Christobel. 'It's too long to read it all, but part of it goes:

Because my sins exceeded the number of the sands of the sea …

I have no strength to lift up my eyes …

for I do not deserve to lift up my eyes

and look to see the height of heaven,

because of the gross iniquity of my wicked deeds …

And now behold I am bending the knees of my heart before

you;

and I am beseeching your kindness …

'There's a whole lot more about how he repents and asks for forgiveness and knows that "you are the God of those who repent/In me you will manifest all your grace", etc. Don't you just love the expression "bending the knees of my heart"?'

'Where's that in the Bible?' demanded Frank.

'It isn't in the Bible, it is in *The Old Testament Pseudepigrapha*, a collection of ancient writings (edited by James Charlesworth) which never made it into the final canon of Scripture,' said Liz. 'It was probably written sometime between the second century BCE and the first century CE.'

'So it's not true,' stated Frank.

'I am afraid that nothing in the Bible indicates that Manasseh ever repented,' said Melinda.

'Perhaps not, but it is a beautiful illustration of divine forgiveness and mercy,' declared Christobel. 'Much better than all that horrid judgement stuff which *is* in the Bible.'

'Uncomfortable though it might be for us, it is important to remember that God is a holy God who cannot abide sin,' reminded Melinda.

'And people who don't obey God like Manasseh end up rotting in hell,' added Frank with relish.

'While there is the judgement theme running through the Deuteronomic history, there is also the theme of God's mercy and compassion,' pointed out Ruth. 'God really did put up with an awful lot from the Israelites. Again and again the Book of Judges describes how the people forsook God and did evil and God punished them by letting their enemies attack them, but then he was moved to pity. It says in 10:16 that "he could no longer bear to see Israel suffer". So he raised up judges to deliver the Israelites from trouble.'

'Like Deborah,' said Christobel enthusiastically, 'who was an amazingly important prophet as well. She'd sit under a palm tree and all the Israelites would come to her to find out what they should do, and she organized their defence against the Canaanites, which just goes to show what a woman can do when given the chance.'

'Yes, and there was also that woman who pretended to be nice and hospitable to one of the Canaanite leaders, and then rammed a tent peg through his head,' said Maureen. 'I expect that he deserved it, but I can't help feeling sorry for his poor mother, waiting at the window, wondering why he didn't come home.'

'That's the tragedy of women caught up in war and violence,' said Christobel with a shudder. 'Forced to use violence to defend themselves, slaughtered and raped, or left to grieve … '

'I didn't like all the stories of wars and people being killed,' confided Kirsty. 'And what I couldn't understand was how God could let wars happen – and not only let wars happen but tell the Israelites when they entered the promised land to kill *every* man, woman, and child living there and show them no mercy!'

'Kirsty, the Canaanites were very, very wicked,' responded Melinda. 'Their whole society was thoroughly degenerate and had to be wiped out.'

'Yeah, they were heavily into perverted sexual practices, incest, bestiality, homosexuality – you name it, they did it,' said Frank. 'Child sacrifice, all that kind of thing. They were much worse than the people of Sodom and Gomorrah, and the people who lived in Noah's time before the Flood, so of course they had to be destroyed ... '

Kirsty looked rather pale.

'It's all right. The massacres didn't really happen,' Wade assured her. 'It was just what the Deuteronomist writing centuries later thought *should* have happened, because he believed that the Israelites had been corrupted by their association with the indigenous inhabitants.'

'Oh,' said Kirsty, not quite sure whether to feel relieved or not.

'As a matter of fact, there are different views of the entry into Canaan in the Bible itself,' continued Wade. 'In Joshua you mostly get the "it was a swift and thorough conquest, thanks to the Lord" version. But in Judges it is clear that the conquest was *not* swift and thorough – many Canaanites remained in the land. Hence some scholars think that it is much more likely that tribes of Israelites immigrated fairly peacefully into Canaan, married Canaanites, bought land, made treaties, and so on, much as they had done in the time of Abraham and Sarah.'

'Which not only ignores the clear biblical account of a major conflict, but also archaeological evidence of destruction consistent with an invasion,' retorted Melinda.

'Oh, we could get into endless debate about archaeological evidence,' said Wade. 'Like everything else, it has to be interpreted, and interpretations differ. But I am not going to defend the peaceful infiltration theory.'

'Thank goodness for that,' said Melinda in mock surprise. 'Will wonders never cease!'

'No,' went on Wade coolly, 'I prefer Gottwald's social revolution theory, which he discusses in his book *The Hebrew*

Bible: A Socio-Literary Introduction. Oppressed Canaanite peasants and disaffected minority groups in society rebelled against the Canaanite city-states, helped by a group of Israelite slaves who had escaped from Egypt with tales about a militant god called "Yahweh".'

'Pure speculation,' said Melinda dismissively.

'Perhaps in some places the Israelites went into battle against the Canaanites and won,' suggested Maureen, 'while in other places they settled fairly peacefully, and occasionally they were helped by revolting peasants.'

'Revolting is the word for them,' muttered Frank.

To Melinda's disgust, Liz agreed that Maureen's theory was quite plausible.

'Did the Jordan River really dry up so that the Israelites could cross it,' asked Kirsty, 'and the walls of Jericho really fall down after the Israelites marched around the city with trumpets? I remember hearing those stories in Sunday School.'

'Yes, they are wonderful accounts of what can happen when people have faith in God and obey his commands,' said Melinda approvingly. 'Obedience was very important because the waters did not actually part until the priests carrying the ark of the covenant stepped into the river. Likewise, the walls did not fall until the people had marched the required number of times around them – and, Kirsty, archaeologists have confirmed that the walls of Jericho did indeed topple down!'

'Well before the Israelites came on to the scene,' scoffed Wade. 'By the time they arrived Jericho was a small, insignificant unwalled settlement. But the interesting thing about the Jericho story is the role played by the Canaanite prostitute, Rahab, who protected the Israelite spies and recognized Yahweh as the true God. There you have an example of how a member of an oppressed minority group in Canaanite society threw her lot in with the Israelites and rebelled against her ruler.'

'I was reading Fretheim's *Deuteronomic History* the other day,' revealed Ruth, 'and he suggests that the story of Jericho's walls falling down reflects liturgy: that the Israelites might have had a ritual ceremony in which they celebrated the conquest of the land.'

'But did it happen?' demanded Maureen.

'Perhaps an earthquake destroyed the walls, and this was re-enacted in the ritual with the trumpet blasts,' answered Ruth. 'But whatever happened, Fretheim says that the point of the story is that it was God who handed the land to the Israelites, they did not have to fight for it. In fact, they met no resistance whatsoever!'

'They just had to go into the city and kill all the women, children, and animals,' spat out Christobel. 'What an absolutely frightful story! Totally incompatible with the God of love revealed by Jesus Christ!'

'War is horrific,' agreed Ruth, 'but it must have been a part of life for the ancient Israelites, necessary for their survival, and if they believed that God was involved in all aspects of their life, they must have believed that that included war.'

'Well, they were wrong,' declared Christobel militantly. 'And the frightful thing is that they set a precedent for future generations of Jewish and Christian fanatics, like the crusaders who committed the most appalling atrocities in the Middle Ages and the European colonists who went off to America, Africa, Australia, New Zealand and so on and ruthlessly seized land from the original inhabitants, murdering many who got in the way. Any murder is absolutely terrible, but when it is presented as the will of God I can't bear it!'

'You cannot blame God if his instructions have sometimes

been misunderstood,' interjected Melinda. 'Those to the Israelites were quite specific. They were not given *carte blanche* to launch holy wars against anyone whatsoever, but only against the people living in the territory which God had promised them at that particular time in history ... '

'And those people had to be wiped out,' reiterated Frank.

'But Wade said that didn't really happen,' objected Maureen, 'didn't you Wade?'

'Yes, but we're just going round in circles,' said Wade in an exasperated tone.

'Perhaps the main issue at stake is whether the Deuteronomic history is, in fact, history,' remarked Liz. 'What do you all think?'

'Joshua, Judges, 1 & 2 Samuel, and 1 & 2 Kings clearly present the history of the Israelites from the conquest of Canaan in the fourteenth century BC through to the fall to Babylon in the sixth century,' replied Melinda firmly.

'But it is not an objective history,' argued Wade, 'there's no such thing, anyway, but the Deuteronomic history is clearly written from the perspective of someone obsessed with the theology of reward and retribution. Be faithful to God and you will be blessed, be unfaithful and you will be cursed. At every major point in Israel's supposed history this is brought up: at the borders of the Promised land (Moses' speech in Deuteronomy 28), at the end of the conquest (Joshua's speech in Joshua 23), at the transition from a confederacy of tribes to a monarchy (Samuel's speech in 1 Samuel 12), and at the dedication of the temple (God's speech to Solomon, 1 Kings 9). The writer has clearly put his theological views into the mouths of Moses, Joshua, Samuel, and God. Then he evaluates the Israelite kings on the basis of whether they "did evil in the sight of the Lord" or "did what was right in the sight of the Lord". He couldn't care less about anything else. If you want to know more about their reigns you are told to go and look up the Book of the Annals of Kings of Israel or the Book of the Annals of the Kings of Judah, which is a great help because they haven't survived!'

'So would you say that it is theology rather than history?' inquired Liz.

Wade nodded.

'And I think it's appalling theology,' cried Christobel. 'A patriarchal warrior god insisting on obedience to his horrid old laws, and punishing the poor people when they inevitably failed … '

'But who often takes pity on them and raises up leaders to help them,' pleaded Ruth, 'judges like Deborah, prophets like Samuel, a king like David. Incidentally, that shows the importance of human leaders, and how God works through them, even if they are imperfect, doesn't it?'

'And the laws aren't all bad,' acknowledged Wade. 'Some of them in Deuteronomy are remarkably humanitarian. Every seven years debts are to be cancelled and slaves set free, enough grain is to be left in the fields after harvest and grapes on the vines for poor people to gather, injured animals must be helped, oxen treading out grain should not be muzzled, a person cannot be convicted of a crime on the evidence of only one person, and so on.'

'Did debts really get cancelled every seven years?' asked Maureen. 'It seems too good to be true. I can just imagine my bank manager agreeing to that deal!'

'Like Crenshaw says in his *Old Testament: Society and Faith*, some of the laws do seem Utopian and out of touch with reality,' replied Wade. 'But that is because they *are* idealistic: what should have happened in retrospect rather than what did happen. The laws with regard to the king are a classic example: he must not acquire many horses, foreign wives, and much silver and gold. Clearly the author wasn't too impressed by Solomon's excesses!'

'As I said last week, I don't think that the law code was meant to be seen as something harsh and legalistic, but as God's gracious gift to the people,' remarked Ruth. 'In Deuteronomy 4:40 Moses says: "Keep his statutes and his commandments, which I am commanding you today *for your own well-being* and that of your descendants after you so that you may long remain in the land that the Lord your God is giving you … " Good laws are necessary for a healthy society. Natural outcomes of obeying them will be life, success and prosperity, while natural outcome of disobeying them will be most unpleasant. That is surely a more nuanced theology than a simple reward/retribution theology: if you obey you will be blessed, and if you disobey you will be cursed.'

'So, in other words, if you take a certain action, you've got to accept that there are consequences,' said Maureen with a sigh. 'That what my old mother reckoned after I married Don: "You've made your bed, Reeny, now you've got to lie on it." She never did want me to marry him. Didn't trust him. She wanted me to marry someone like Bruce, my cousin Dorothy's boyfriend. Bruce was her idea of a model of respectability. He worked in his father's plumbing firm, never drank or smoked, and his only form of recreation was going to meetings of the camera club and singing in the church choir. My Don was the complete opposite. Smoked like a train, drank like a fish, never set foot near a church if he could help it, hung out at night clubs, and was a used car salesman! He was a damn good one, too. There was nothing Don couldn't sell. Mother used to reckon that he'd have sold his grandmother if she hadn't died before he was born.

'Well, to cut a long story short, Dorothy married Boring

Bruce, and I married Dashing Don. Boring Bruce is still a model of respectability, he still sings in the church choir, and he still belongs to some benighted camera club. His family business has been so successful that now he's semi-retired, and able to take Dorothy on overseas trips. Their latest jaunt was to Australia. They came to dinner last Saturday with their projector and screen and inflicted their Ayers Rock collection on me. It was incredible! Bruce had stood in one place for hours and hours, clicking every thirty seconds so that he would have a record of how the rock changed colour as the sun changed position. I don't know how many hundreds of slides I ended up seeing. Every so often Bruce would say, "I'll skip the next twenty," but it didn't seem to make much difference. If I ever manage to get to Australia myself, at least I can cross Ayers Rock off my itinerary. I never want to see the wretched thing again.'

'Can we get back to the Deuteronomic history?' said Wade impatiently.

'Yes, I know I'm waffling again, but the point is,' hurried on Maureen, 'that Boring Bruce has provided Dorothy with a life of comfort and ease, while Dashing Don has dashed off with his secretary and left me with next to nothing! I made my choice almost thirty years ago, and now I've got to live with the consequences.'

'But, Maureen, do you really think that you would have been happier married to Bruce?' asked Christobel earnestly. 'He does sound frightfully boring, and if he was a plumber, you'd never – you know – know where his hands had been!'

'I never knew where Don's hands had been, if it comes to that, but I must admit, you're right, Christobel. If I had my life all over again, I'm sure I'd probably choose another Don. Dorothy can keep Bruce and her six toilets. That's another thing that's incredible. Apart from an *en suite* for every bedroom, there's one in the laundry, one off the pool room, even one in the garden shed. Every time I visit, I find that Bruce has put in another as a present for Dorothy. But who'd want to clean that many? It's ridiculous now that the kids have left home and she and Bruce are on their own ... '

'Any more questions or comments about the Deuteronomic history?' asked Liz.

'Yes, I've got a question,' said Maureen. 'Who was the Deuterowhatnot person who wrote it all down, anyway?'

'Nobody knows,' answered Melinda scornfully. 'Liberal scholars just come up with theories, theories, endless conflicting theories.'

'Nicholson suggests in his book *Deuteronomy and Tradition* that traditions about Moses were preserved among circles of prophets in northern Israel,' said Ruth. 'Some of them may have fled south to Judah when the northern kingdom collapsed in 721. During Manasseh's wicked reign they could have drawn up a programme of reform (an early form of the Book of Deuteronomy) and placed it in the temple where it was discovered when Josiah became king, and it became the basis for the Josianic reform. The "Deuteronomic" circle then revived during Josiah's time, played an active part in the reform, and after the downfall of Judah produced the Deuteronomic history.'

'Do you agree that the Deuteronomic history could have originated in prophetic circles?' asked Liz.

'I think it is a plausible suggestion,' Ruth answered slowly. 'Nicholson mentions the affinities between the concerns of Deuteronomy and those of the prophet Hosea who addressed the northern kingdom in the eighth century, but, most of all, Moses himself is described as a prophet in Deuteronomy 18:18, and in the following "history books" the role of prophets as intercessors and spokesmen of God's word is continually highlighted. There are the wonderful stories of the great prophets Elijah and Elisha in 1 Kings and … '

'But if you actually read Deuteronomy,' interrupted Wade, 'the group which comes out on top again and again is not the prophets but the priests from the tribe of Levi. They are the ones given direct access to Yahweh in 10:8, and in 17:8 they are given the final say in all disputes and the interpretation of the law. Anyone who presumes to disobey them is to be put to death! Even kings have to live according to the law interpreted by the Levites!'

'And this could only have been written by Levites! Must we be so cynical?' asked Melinda.

'It's not being cynical,' replied Wade, 'just logical. If you want to know who is responsible for a document, consider whose interests are being served by it. That's what Gottwald does, and he concludes that it was the Levites who were most likely to have been the "bearers of the traditions" in Deuteronomy. However, he also acknowledges that they could have co-operated with court officials during the reigns of Hezekiah and Josiah, and they were doubtless influenced by the eighth-century prophets Amos, Hosea, Micah, and Isaiah who promoted socio-economic justice.'

'So we're not looking for just one author-person, but a whole group,' said Maureen, thinking aloud. 'Levites and court officials who were interested in prophecy and liked preaching boring sermons about the need to be faithful to Yahweh. Well, that narrows the field down a bit.'

'What you're really saying is that Deuteronomy's a fraud,' declared Frank angrily, 'because it wasn't written by Moses. But Jesus thought Moses was the author, and that's good enough for me!'

'I didn't say that it was fraud', said Ruth. 'I was putting forward Nicholson's theory that it comes from prophetic circles from the northern kingdom, who preserved traditions about Moses that had been passed on to them. Wade was saying that it was more likely levitical circles that passed on the traditions that they had received. In either case, the traditions could have been very ancient, and those responsible for passing them on could have thought that they were genuine. However, the final editing, if not the actual writing of the Deuteronomic history, must have been accomplished while the Israelites were in exile in Babylon.'

'The Babylonians can't have treated them too badly then,' reflected Maureen, 'because it wasn't only the Deuterthingy history that got finished off. Didn't priests in exile put together the Pentateuch, too?'

'Yes,' agreed Wade. 'The Israelites had considerable freedom to engage in social, economic and literary activities. It was a very productive period.'

'It must also have been a very challenging period,' stressed Ruth. 'The Israelites would have been exposed to Babylonian culture and religious traditions. Some Israelites must have been very concerned about this and the danger that their own religious traditions would be swamped by those of Babylon and forgotten. There was a great need to preserve the traditions and pass them on to following generations. This comes out very strongly in Deuteronomy:

Take care and watch yourselves closely, so as neither to forget the things that your eyes have seen nor to let them slip from your mind all the days of your life; make them known to your children and your children's children – how you once stood before the Lord your God at Horeb ... (Deuteronomy 4:9–10)

Hear, O Israel: The Lord is our God, the Lord alone. You shall love the Lord your God with all your heart, and with all your soul, and with all your might. Keep these words that I am commanding you today in your heart. Recite them to your children and talk about them when you are at home and when you are away, when you lie down and when you rise. Bind them as a sign on your hand, fix them as an emblem on your forehead, and write them on the doorposts of your house and on your gates ... (Deuteronomy 6:4–9)

'I also think that Deuteronomy has been very cleverly written so that future generations can feel that Moses is speaking to them,' continued Ruth, her voice filled with enthusiasm. '"The Lord our God made a covenant with us at Horeb. Not with our ancestors did the Lord make this covenant, but with *us*, who are all of us here alive today ... "' (Deuteronomy 5:2–3). Dennis Olson says on page 16 of his *Deuteronomy and the Death of Moses: A Theological Reading* that "the past is recalled in order to shape the present life of the community and in order to thrust the community always toward the future, both a future near at hand and a future more distant. The community of faith is rooted in the past, active in the present, but always open to and yearning for God's new future." I am sorry if I am boring you with this, but I have just finished looking at Deuteronomy in my essay, and it strikes me as so important. It is what Christians have to do too: pass on cherished traditions to following generations, making them relevant to contemporary concerns ... '

At this point Dave wandered casually into the room. He said that he was sorry that he was late but he had had to finish off his essay and his printer had run out of ink, so he'd had to go to the shops.

'Now that you are here, is there anything that you would like to contribute about the Deuteronomic history before we finish up?' asked Liz rather acidly.

'Deut history? Um … I was actually too busy with my essay on Genesis to do any reading on that, but it's great stuff, isn't it? Pity poor old Moses isn't around to collect the royalties.'

'Most of the Deuteronomic history deals with things which happened long after Moses snuffed it,' pointed out Jason.

'Yes, the rest was written by … er … Joshua, Judges, Samuel, and … er … whoever wrote Kings,' went on Dave vaguely. 'What great books they are! All those wonderful things God did for the Israelites! Like when he made the walls of Jericho fall down. I remember that from Sunday School. We used to march around the room and I got to play my trumpet … '

'I remember it being taught at Sunday School, too,' said Kirsty eagerly, 'but we never had a trumpet.'

'Oh, we did,' continued Dave, 'and tambourines. It made a heck of a racket, but it was great fun.'

Liz gave up.

'Dave and Kirsty can continue reminiscing if they want too,' she said, 'but I have to go now. Have a good mid-semester break!'

'Will try to. I sure am ready for a holiday,' exclaimed Dave. 'It's been a really tough term. Want to come to the refectory for a drink, Kirsty?'

Kirsty turned pink with pleasure and went off with him.

The rest of us sat slumped in our chairs, too exhausted and dumbfounded to move.

WEEK·SEVEN

Job

First day back after the mid-semester break and we had to wrestle with Job. Everyone arrived on time except Dave, who couldn't join us because he was on a soccer training camp.

'Would anyone like to hazard a guess as to the date of the Book of Job?' asked Liz to get us started.

'It's very old,' replied Melinda firmly. 'Job serves as a priest in his own house so it must have been written before the priesthood and the temple were established, and there is no reference to the Exodus, so it probably dates from the time before Moses.'

'Rubbish,' retorted Wade. 'The literary setting of the book may be the dim, distant past, but the author was doubtless writing for the Israelites during or after the Babylonian exile. They must have been struggling to come to terms with the issue of why the "righteous" were suffering and the "wicked" were prospering, contrary to the doctrine of reward and retribution spelt out by the Deuteronomic historian and some of the prophets: do good and you will be blessed, do evil and you will suffer.'

Melinda looked coldly at him.

'I hardly think that the problem of suffering was confined to the fifth and sixth centuries!'

'And the prophet Ezekiel mentions Job as one of the

patriarchs along with Noah,' pointed out Frank. 'So you must be right, Melinda.'

'Another view held by some scholars,' intervened Ruth, 'seems to be that the prose prologue and epilogue, which describe the heavenly court scene where God and Satan decide to test Job, his afflictions, his initial response, and the eventual restoration of his wealth, is actually a very old folk-tale, to which the poetic dialogues in the middle were added at a much later date. So perhaps Melinda and Wade are both right.'

'Job is one of the books in the Bible which are impossible to date,' said Liz with a nod. 'But it is quite likely that more than one author or editor contributed to it.'

'Likely? It is obvious to anyone with half a brain!' declared Wade. 'There is such a dramatic change from the passive Job of the prologue who accepts the trials which befall him to the aggressive Job of the dialogues who seeks vindication. And the "and they all lived happily ever after" ending is such an anti-climax after the profound sense of mystery and paradox raised by the dialogues.'

'Actually, I like a happy ending,' confided Kirsty.

'So do I!' agreed Maureen. 'They might not be considered sophisticated or arty, but I want to read books that make me feel good. There's enough in real life to make me depressed and frustrated – that's what I want to escape from when I read. So now I rarely bother with new books, I stick to old favourites, like Agatha Christie novels. There's nothing like a good murder mystery for a real good read, and with Agatha Christie you know that Miss Marple or Hercule Poirot will find the killer in the end and all will be revealed.'

Ruth admitted to being an Agatha Christie fan too, but tried to point out that when she suggested that parts of Job might have been written at different times, she didn't mean to imply that they are completely separate. 'I think that they have been very cleverly woven together,' she explained. 'Norman Habel shows in the introduction to his commentary on Job that there is a coherent plot which extends right through the book from the prologue to the epilogue. Thus, "the chief character of the plot is tested, suffers great anguish, stands alone, defies heaven, and emerges a true hero".'

'Yes,' sighed Christobel. 'It really is a literary masterpiece. Tennyson once called it the greatest poem in ancient and modern literature!'

Maureen looked sceptical.

'Well, to be honest, I thought that it went on for too long. I tried to read it last night in one sitting but I kept dozing off.'

I admitted that I had a similar experience.

'But that's part of the literary plot,' insisted Christobel. 'Job's so-called friends drone on with their tired old arguments, and end up getting nowhere.'

'They certainly succeeded in boring me,' said Jason with a yawn.

'Perhaps it would be more interesting if we considered the main characters one by one,' said Liz brightly. 'Who were they?'

'There is Job, obviously,' answered Melinda. 'It says in the first verse that he was "blameless and upright, one who feared God and turned away from evil". His initial (and most commendable) response to the calamities which befell him was to worship God and say: "Naked I came from my mother's womb, and naked I shall return there: the Lord gave and the Lord has taken away; blessed be the name of the Lord."'

'What a pain in the neck,' muttered Maureen.

'Clearly, the overall purpose of the book is to show the

proper relationship between man and God,' continued Melinda. 'Man must respond to God in faith and submissive trust.'

'Even when your entire family has just been wiped out?' cried Christobel.

'I don't know how I'd cope if I had 10 kids who were all suddenly killed,' admitted Maureen frankly, 'but I think I'd find faith and trust in pretty short supply.'

'I'm afraid that I would too,' said Liz. 'What about some of the other characters?'

'There is Satan,' said Frank in a low voice, 'sneering, insolent, pacing the earth seeking victims to devour ... '

Kirsty shuddered.

'"Satan",' retorted Wade, 'is not a personal name but a role specification. *The* Satan (the word means accuser or adversary) was clearly in Yahweh's service – a sort of roving spy or intelligence officer. It was his duty to report back to Yahweh what was going on on earth, just as spies were employed by Persian kings in the ancient world to check out was going on in their dominions.'

'You know, it really struck me while I was reading the story last night,' remarked Ruth, 'that it is actually Yahweh who directs the Satan's attention to Job, not the other way around.'

'And God or Yahweh or whatever his name is boasts about how good Job is,' added Maureen. 'As a matter of fact, I don't think that Satan was being particularly nasty when he pointed out that it wasn't surprising that Job praised God, because God had blessed him so much. He was just being realistic. And God didn't have to agree immediately to his suggestion that they should take away all of Job's blessings to find out whether he would then curse God or not. Apparently God couldn't resist a bet. My father was just the same. He would bet on anything, even two flies going up a wall. What my poor mother had to put up with!'

Christobel sympathized with her and agreed that she thought that God didn't come across frightfully well in the prologue: as well as being boastful and easily provoked, when Job passed the first test with flying colours, God turned on the Satan and accused him of inciting him for no reason.

'Then, of course, another character is Job's wife,' continued Maureen. 'Like my poor old mother, she must have had a lot to put up with too. I can sure understand her getting fed up and telling Job to curse God and die.'

'Alas, like Eve, she was the devil's advocate,' said Frank grimly.

Christobel glared at him.

'According to the Testament of Job her name was Sitis, and Job spent 48 years moping on his dung heap outside the city walls while she had to work her fingers to the bone as a slave in a nobleman's house,' Christobel said in a voice throbbing with emotion. 'She barely got enough food for herself but she shared everything with Job. She even had to resort to begging in the market place, and she sold her hair to buy bread for him – and if a woman had short hair back then it was a sign of disgrace. Finally, after 48 years of this, she could bear it no longer and she begged Job to curse God and die. But that self-righteous, lazy, masochistic, good-for-nothing, maggot-ridden, pain-in-the-neck actually rebuked her and told her to be patient! Patient! After 48 years!'

'Where did you find that?' asked Frank, flicking through his Bible in bewilderment. 'Job's wife only gets two verses in my edition.'

'Typical! Typical!' cried Christobel. 'As usual the role of women is downgraded in the patriarchal mainstream tradition!'

Liz pointed out that the Testament of Job is in *The Old Testament Pseudepigrapha*, the collection of ancient writings (edited by James Charlesworth) which never made it into the final canon of Scripture. The Testament of Job was probably written in the first century BCE or CE. If it is not very historically reliable, it does, nevertheless, show that different stories were circulating about Job in the ancient world. And,' continued Liz, 'although Job's wife only gets such a brief mention in the official version, she does have an important role. She raises one of the key issues in the book – is it better to give in, curse God, and die, or persevere and suffer?'

'Well, in chapter 3 Job does let off steam by cursing the day he was born,' observed Maureen. 'A pretty long-winded curse it is, too. He basically just seems to be saying: "I wish I was dead." I know that's what I thought when my husband left me.'

'And Job's curse is the catalyst which prods his so-called "friends" into speaking,' observed Wade.

'Yes. What did you think of the friends?' asked Liz.

'Eliphaz, the first friend to speak, genuinely sympathizes with Job,' remarked Melinda. 'He respectfully suggests what he would do in Job's place: "As for me, I would seek God and to God I would commit my cause." That is still very good advice, and he quite rightly exhorts Job to have faith and be patient.'

'He is smug and complacent, and just mouths conventional religious platitudes!' exploded Wade. 'The innocent will never perish, God frustrates the designs of the wicked, he saves the poor and needy – what comfort is that to someone who has just had his family wiped out?'

'And he raves on about "how happy is the one whom God reproves",' said Christobel angrily, 'as if Job and his family's enormous, absolutely dreadful suffering is merely some sort of fatherly correction. I think that that is absolutely appalling theology!'

'You can learn a great deal from times of suffering,' reminded Melinda.

'Oh, I know,' exclaimed Christobel. 'You can discover depths of yourself that you never knew existed, you can become much more mature, and all that, but Job's suffering is surely out of all proportion to anything that he could possibly learn from it!'

'Yes. Well, I certainly learned a lot from the experience of my divorce,' contributed Maureen. 'I can stand on my own feet, now. Before I couldn't even change a light bulb or pay an electricity bill. But, while I had to learn to get by without Don and my lovely home and financial security, I didn't lose my kids, thank God. They still supported me. I think I would've gone mad if they'd all died, like Job's did.'

'Job needs to be able to articulate his grief,' said Ruth earnestly. 'It is welling up inside him and can't be contained, but the friends are horrified and try to hush him up.'

'They gave better pastoral care in chapter 2 when they just sat with him for seven days and nights and kept their mouths shut,' said Wade.

'As it says in Ecclesiastes, there is a time to mourn, a time to weep, a time to keep silence … ' murmured Liz.

'Yes,' agreed Ruth. 'And I think that we do people who are suffering a great disservice if we do not let them have that time.'

'The trouble is, people don't really want to hear other people's problems,' reflected Maureen. 'When my husband left me my best friend Enid kept trying to think up ways to "cheer me up" – like going to Weight Watchers or having my hair coloured. All I wanted was a shoulder to cry on. And another one of my chief gripes is that whenever anyone greets anybody else, it's always "How are you today?". You can't get out of the supermarket without the assistant behind the counter saying "How are you today?" But how many people really want to find out how you really are? I always end up saying "Fine, thanks," even if I'm feeling terrible, because that's what people expect to hear.'

'It's automatic,' said Liz with a nod. 'Job, however, decides to be honest: "Therefore I will not restrain my mouth; I will speak in the anguish of my spirit; I will complain in the bitterness of my soul." So how does Bildad, the next character on the scene, respond?'

'He lays into Job for losing his temper, reckons that no way does God pervert justice, and implies that Job's kids' deaths were punishment for their sins!' answered Jason. 'A great comfort that would have been!'

'Now, that would really have made me mad if I was Job,' exclaimed Maureen. 'When my son Neil was hurt in a motor bike accident (he wasn't killed, thank God, he just broke a few bones and was badly bruised) Enid invited herself into my kitchen for a cup of tea and went on and on about how inconsiderate Neil was to worry me like he did, and it served him right for falling off his bike, and she hoped it would teach him a lesson. Well, I was real put out! The fact that I'd been saying exactly the same things to my daughter half an hour before was totally irrelevant. It's all right for me to criticize my kids – but I am not going to sit back and listen to anybody else do so. Some people just have no tact! I had to look at hundreds of photos of Enid's fat daughter's wedding and say how beautiful she looked, but when she saw my Gail's photos it was, "Oh, why on earth did you let her choose that dress? ... I must say that I don't think that style suits her ... "'

'Job's friends certainly weren't very tactful,' said Liz, adroitly managing to get the conversation back to Job. 'But what do you think really lies behind their responses to his plight?'

'They all assume that God governs the world with order and justice, and that virtue will be rewarded and wickedness punished,' responded Wade. 'Hence, the best that they can say to Job is that if he is innocent, he will be delivered from his suffering.'

'But they become more and more convinced that his suffering is *proof* of his wickedness,' exclaimed Christobel, 'and that he should repent of whatever it is that he has done.'

'It must be one of the most terrible things in life to be unjustly accused of some kind of wrongdoing,' said Ruth quietly, 'and to know that even your friends doubt your innocence.'

'Of course, Job is initially operating out of the same belief system,' Wade swept on. 'His point is that he knows that he is innocent, that he has done nothing to deserve the suffering, so the fact that he has received suffering instead of blessing raises a huge question mark over God's ability to govern the world with justice. He accuses God of being his enemy, and wants to bring a legal suit against him so that he can be proved innocent in court. Even though he knows that it is hopeless, he prepares his case and challenges God to do likewise.'

'Which is incredibly foolish, arrogant, and presumptuous,' declared Melinda.

'Yes,' said Wade with a wry smile, 'that's exactly what the pious friends think, and as a result they become increasingly hostile to Job, who becomes increasingly alienated from them.'

'The trouble with the friends,' explained Melinda, 'is that they expected rewards and punishment to be manifest in *this* life. We know that we have to wait to Judgement Day.'

'We need to have faith. That's the whole point of the book,' affirmed Frank. 'It's ridiculous for Job to try to make God answer charges because it is Job, not God, who is on trial to see how strong his faith really is.'

'The theology of the friends is still very powerful in some churches,' observed Wade dryly.

'It certainly is!' agreed Christobel. 'I have a friend who went to a Pentecostal church where the pastor used to say things like: "You can tell who are putting the most money in the collection plate because they're the ones with the new cars parked in the car park." In other words, the more you give to the church, the more prosperous you'll be! That sort of preaching was bad enough, but it got even worse when poor Dianne found that she had cancer. The whole church prayed and prayed for her but no miraculous cure took place, so people started looking for reasons: perhaps she didn't have enough faith, or there was a demon inside her, or she hadn't repented of some secret sin. It was Job's case all over again! Absolutely incredible! And, like Job, she got really angry and bitter, because at a time in her life when she really needed comfort, all she got was accusations. Needless to say, eventually she left the church.'

'If there is one certainty in life,' commented Liz, 'it is that sooner or later we all come up against some form of pain and suffering, and it is suffering that poses one of the greatest challenges to belief in the existence of God. As philosopher David Hume once wrote: "Is God willing to prevent evil, but not able? Then he is impotent. Is he able, but not willing? Then he is malevolent. Is he both able and willing? Whence then is evil?" So what "answers" (if any) to this conundrum do you get from the Book of Job?'

'A person can triumph over suffering through faith in God,' stated Melinda with calm certainty. 'God had not abandoned

Job, even though it sometimes seemed to Job that he had.'

'1 Corinthians 10: "God is faithful and he will not let you be tested beyond your strength",' quoted Frank joyfully.

'And while Job succumbed to anger and pride, he also had a prophetic glimpse of the Atonement, the Incarnation, and the Resurrection,' continued Melinda. 'As he says in 19:25, "For I know that my Redeemer lives, and that at the last he will stand upon the earth; and after my skin has been thus destroyed, then in my flesh I shall see God … "'

'The "redeemer" mentioned in verse 19 isn't Christ,' said Wade with a sigh. 'In keeping with the legal terminology running through the book, it just means that Job is convinced that, in spite of his skin disease, before he dies someone will take up his case and defend him. There is no other indication in the book that the characters believed in the possibility of resurrection from the dead: quite the contrary.'

'Naturally, because the wonderful doctrines of the Atonement, the Incarnation, and Resurrection did not become clear until the fuller revelation of God in the Word made flesh,' replied Melinda, 'but there are still glimpses of them in the Old Testament, as in Job 19.'

'Well, if the redeemer isn't Christ, who is he?' asked Maureen reasonably.

'Perhaps God himself?' suggested Ruth.

'But Job has just been carrying on about God being his enemy,' pointed out Wade, 'and he keeps up that train of thought after making the redeemer statement.'

'If the Satan can pop up in the court of heaven as Job's accuser, I don't see why another angel couldn't pop up to defend him – preferably a female one with more compassion,' said Christobel.

'But it doesn't say anything about that in the Bible,' objected Frank.

'And it is God who appears to Job in the whirlwind at the end of the book,' said Melinda.

'And a big help that is, too,' said Maureen sarcastically. 'Redeemer? He's pompous, overbearing, arrogant and insensitive, and he doesn't answer any of Job's questions. That might be your idea of a redeemer, but it sure isn't mine.'

'God doesn't need to answer Job's questions,' maintained Melinda. 'Job has been guilty of great arrogance and presumption in demanding answers. His faith was too small to cover the contingency of innocent suffering. He had to project the blame for his suffering onto God. God appears in the whirlwind as a holy, righteous, and just God who is beyond our comprehension. If he permits the wicked to prosper it must be because he wants to give everyone a chance to repent. He allows evil to exist in the short term so that in the long term he can reveal his grace. However, no evil is ultimately beyond his control. Much of the Book of Job cannot be regarded as authoritative divine teaching (although all the characters except Satan speak elements of truth), but God's speech clearly is.'

'So it's authoritative divine teaching that mythical creatures like the leviathan and the behemoth really exist,' said Jason with a glint in his eye. 'God definitely mentions them!'

'Leviathan and behemoth are obviously ancient names for the hippopotamus and crocodile,' replied Melinda.

'Or whales and elephants,' said Frank.

'Really?' asked Jason, fascinated. 'So how do you explain the fact that Psalm 74 says that leviathan are multi-headed? What a novelty that would be at the zoo! A multi-headed hippopotamus or whale!'

Wade gave a sarcastic laugh.

'The character "God" speaks from the whirlwind in *poetic* language,' stressed Liz, 'which surely means that his words are not necessarily meant to be taken literally. So do you still think that the "answer" of the Book of Job to the problem of innocent suffering is humble submission to God?'

Melinda and Frank nodded.

'But Job didn't humbly submit!' cried out Christobel, bouncing up and down in her chair in frustration. 'He was frightfully brave and *challenged* God!'

'Yes, but he later repented of his arrogance,' said Melinda. 'Chapter 42, verse 6: " … therefore I despise myself, and repent in dust and ashes".'

'I think that Habel's translation is different,' said Ruth, flicking through the book. 'Here it is: " … therefore I retract and repent *of* dust and ashes".'

'He retracts his lawsuit against God, and he decides to get off the ash heap and go back to normal life,' concluded Wade.

'It is a very difficult verse to translate,' said Liz. '"Dust" and "ashes" is pretty straightforward, but the verb which Habel translates "retract" and the NRSV "despise" has no object; and the Hebrew word which has traditionally been translated "in" (as in "I repent in … ") could equally validly be translated "of", "from", "concerning", or "about".'

'The context should govern the translation, not pious tradition,' maintained Wade. 'The book loses its point if Job has to repent! God proclaims at the very beginning that Job is blameless and upright. The friends believe that Job's demand to confront God with his lawsuit is incredibly presumptuous and God will never appear (after all, in Hebrew tradition a mortal couldn't see God and live, unless he or she was someone exceptional like Moses) – but, lo and behold, God does appear to Job and he lives to tell the tale! God's appearance vindicates Job, and despite Job's angry words against God, it is the *friends* whom God rebukes. They are told in no uncertain terms that they have not spoken correctly of God while

Job has. And it is Job who has to intercede on their behalf to deliver them from God's wrath!'

'So the moral of the story is that it is OK to get angry with God, to be honest, and pour out your complaints,' said Christobel enthusiastically. 'God is big enough to handle it!'

'But is there any answer to the problem of evil and suffering?' asked Liz, glancing at her watch.

Wade shook his head, then said, 'However, God's speeches from the whirlwind do make it quite clear that there is no system of reward and retribution built into the running of the universe. The universe is *amoral*.'

'And that is one of the reasons,' commented Liz, 'why Tsevat, in his article "The Meaning of Job" (in the book *Sitting with Job: Selected Studies on the Book of Job*, edited by Roy Zuck), says that Job is the most daring and radical of biblical books.'

'I like the way that Habel shows that God highlights the paradoxical nature of the world in the whirlwind speeches,' said Ruth. 'There is good and evil, life and death, order and chaos, freedom and control, wisdom and folly. But, while there is no simplistic answer to the problem of innocent suffering, God is always there, watching over and caring for creation, and God sometimes intervenes to balance the conflicting forces and aid the weak and helpless.'

'And God makes Job prosperous again at the end,' said Kirsty eagerly.

'Doesn't that mean that we get back to the old "the righteous will be blessed" argument?' asked Maureen.

'I think that Job's restoration just shows God's amazing generosity,' said Ruth. 'After all, he got twice as many animals as he had before … '

'And he had seven more sons and three more absolutely beautiful daughters and he "*gave them an inheritance along with their brothers*",' enthused Christobel, 'which was incredibly rare in those times. What must have happened was that while he was awful to his wife in chapter 2, he learned as time went by to value women more.'

'Any final comments?' asked Liz.

'I find it extremely ironic,' said Wade, 'that although Job must have been written by someone who was pretty hacked off with the orthodox teaching of his day, orthodoxy has almost always won out in translations and interpretations of the book!'

Frank glared at him and muttered something incoherent.

'I suppose that we've just got to live with the fact that good people suffer,' reflected Maureen. 'Little kids die, people get accused of crimes they didn't commit, husbands walk out on their wives for younger women. I'm torn between wishing that God would intervene a bit more to help people and liking my freedom too.'

Liz nodded.

'We must stop now,' she concluded, 'but don't forget that Job is a literary work, a drama, *not* a philosophical or theological treatise. Be very wary of books and commentaries which try to show that it has a packaged answer to the problem of innocent suffering, because there isn't one there. It's something we all have to wrestle with.'

'But we can take a leaf out of Job's book and be brave, be honest, and not take any notice of false comforters,' declared Maureen stoutly. 'Now if I'd done that when my husband left me …'

WEEK·EIGHT

Psalms

Dave turned up today, collapsed into a chair, and said that he hadn't done any reading for our discussion. He'd been too whacked. His soccer training camp finished with a 25-mile marathon. He came third. If we didn't believe him, he'd show us the blisters on his feet. Liz, with a glance at the battered Reebok waved in front of her, said that we'd take his word for it. Kirsty also apologized for not doing any reading. She had been too upset last night. Tweetie Pie, her budgie, is dead.

'You poor thing! What happened?' asked Christobel sympathetically.

'I thought that it was cruel to keep him shut up in his little cage all day long,' she said with a quaver in her voice, 'so I let him fly around my room. He really loved it, and he would fly back to me and hop on my shoulder when ever I clapped ... '

'You were absolutely right to let him fly,' Christobel assured her. 'I hate seeing birds cooped up in little cages all the time. But what went wrong?'

It turned out that the lady who owns the house where Kirsty boards opened the window to air the room while Kirsty was out, not realizing that little Tweetie Pie was loose, and Tweetie Pie made his escape.

'Well, you never know, he might turn up again, or someone

could find him,' said Maureen encouragingly. 'Put a notice in the local paper.'

'Oh,' said Kirsty tearfully, 'I went around to all the houses in the neighbourhood last night, asking if anyone had seen a budgie, and someone *had* found him – or what remained of him – left on the back doormat by the cat!'

Christobel gave her a hug.

'That's the trouble with pets, sooner or later they die,' said Maureen. 'I had no end of trouble when my kids were little. I forget the number of birds, fish, and frogs we got through.'

'I am very sorry, Kirsty, that your budgie is dead,' said Liz, 'but do you think we could get started now?'

Kirsty wiped her eyes and nodded.

'OK, today we are supposed to consider the fact that although the psalms are written as human praise or prayer to God, we still speak of them as part of God's revelation,' said Liz in a brisk tone. 'So in what sense can they be said to reveal God to humanity?'

'Of course the psalms are part of God's revelation,' contributed Frank, 'they must be because they are in the Bible.'

'But they are not the words of God to the Israelites – they are the words of the Israelites to God,' pointed out Wade.

'All Scripture is inspired by God, it says so itself,' retorted Frank. '2 Timothy 3:16 … '

'Oh no, here we go again,' muttered Wade.

'As I have said before, the miracle of Scripture is that God could communicate his infallible revelation through fallible men,' maintained Melinda. 'Just as God used Moses to reveal the Pentateuch, and Solomon the wisdom literature, he used David to reveal the psalms.'

'No serious scholar still believes in Davidic authorship,' scoffed Wade.

'Nineteenth-century liberal scholars tried to prove that most psalms originated centuries after David in the second century BC or thereabouts, but it is now increasingly recognized that they are much older,' argued Melinda.

'Yes,' said Wade with a gleam in his eyes. 'In 1928 an Arab peasant stumbled across the ruins of the ancient city of Ugarit in Syria, and archaeologists have uncovered dozens of clay tablets dating from about 1375–1340 BCE. These reveal that ancient Canaanites used words, phrases, and poetic structures which are very similar to those found in the psalms. Clearly, therefore, the Israelites and the Canaanites had a shared cultural tradition, so it is not surprising that scholars suspect that Psalm 29 was originally written as a hymn to the Canaanite god Baal, and was later adapted for the worship of Yahweh. In the Ugaritic texts Baal is manifest in thunder, lightening, and storm (as Yahweh is in Psalm 29), and if you substitute "Baal" for "Yahweh" in the Hebrew text many alliterations appear. A Canaanite background for the psalm would also explain why the first verse implies a polytheistic context in which there are "sons of gods".'

'They're just theories,' Frank struck back, 'but the Bible itself says that Psalm 29 and many other psalms were written by David, like Psalm 51 which he wrote after he sinned with Bathsheba and had her husband Uriah killed.'

'The headings and notes that you are referring to were added by pre-Christian Jewish scribes long after the psalms were written,' responded Wade dismissively. 'Some might give clues to authorship but most probably represent the unhistorical assumptions of later generations. It is almost universally accepted that Psalm 51 was composed during or shortly after the Babylonian exile in the sixth century. It reflects the awareness of sin which emerged in that period, begs Yahweh to "rebuild the walls of Jerusalem" (which had been destroyed when Judah was conquered), and says "against you, you alone, have I sinned" with no reference to poor old Uriah!'

'Frank, it is certainly possible that David wrote some of the psalms,' intervened Liz, 'but, as Wade said, the tradition that he wrote half of them arose relatively late. Did any of you read anything else that struck you as interesting about the dates and original purposes of the psalms?'

'Psalm 45 may have been composed for the wedding of Ahab and Jezebel,' said Jason with a grin. 'Wasn't she the one who persecuted the prophet Elijah, pinched somebody's vineyard, and got eaten by dogs? Whoever wrote the psalm was certainly right that her husband's memory would be perpetuated through all generations, but he got the being praised for ever and ever a bit wrong.'

'Of course, the sources we have are doubtless biased against Jezebel because she was a woman,' said Christobel. 'I expect that if we could really get to know her we'd find that she was quite nice. And even if she did make a few mistakes (who doesn't?) I'm sure that she didn't deserve to be thrown out the window, trampled by horses, and eaten by dogs. How absolutely horrid! But what I was going to say was that I was absolutely fascinated to find that my favourite psalm, Psalm 139, may have arisen as a public declaration of innocence which people made when they were accused of idol worship. That's why it starts off, "O Lord, you have searched me and known me", and ends with those horrid bits about hating God's enemies.'

Ruth revealed that she had read that some psalms, like Psalm 121, may have been sung by pilgrims on the road to Jerusalem, and others, such as Psalm 15, may have been used as part of the rite of entrance to the temple.

Mention of the temple made me remember that I had read that a number of psalms (including one of my favourites,

Psalm 100) may have been used in a 'cultic enthronement of Yahweh' ceremony. I tried to explain how Mowinckel, one of the scholars who dominated psalm scholarship earlier this century, believed that the Israelites may have had such a ceremony in which Yahweh's rule over the earth was proclaimed and cultically renewed.

Liz gave me an encouraging smile, but Melinda retorted that Mowinckel's theory has by no means been accepted by all scholars, and she has better things to do with her time than waste it on idle speculation. She also couldn't see what relevance endless controversies among liberal scholars about how the psalms originated have to the ordinary Christian in the pew.

'Well, speaking as an ordinary pew person, I think that it is really interesting that Psalm 45 might have written for Abab and Jezebel,' said Maureen, 'but I suppose that in the long run it doesn't matter all that much. It's the same with hymns in our hymnbook. Take that one by Whatshisname ... '

At this point, Maureen broke into song, slightly off-key:

'O Love that wilt not let me go,
Tra la la la la la la la la,
Mm mm mm mm mm mm mm mm mm,
that in thine ocean depths its flow
may richer, fuller be ...

'You'd never guess that I've been asked to join the choir, would you? Shows how desperate they are for new members, but I'm too busy studying to have time to go to choir practice, even if I could sing, and I don't want to commit myself to going to church every week. Now what got me on to that? Oh, yes, my minister said once, when he was announcing that hymn, that whatshisname wrote it after he went blind, or his fiancée left him, or his wife died, or some such thing. Which is very sad, of course, but the point is, people will still be singing it long after he's dead and the circumstances in which he wrote it are forgotten. And that's exactly what's happened with the psalms!'

Maureen finished on a pleased note.

'Yes,' agreed Liz with a laugh. 'OK, to sum up so far, I think that we can safely say that the psalms were composed by many different people, over many centuries, for many different purposes ... '

Frank folded his arms and Melinda pursed her lips in a disapproving way.

'And that makes our question today all the more important,' Liz hurried on. 'How did the Psalter come to be considered part of God's revelation?'

'Actually, as far as I am concerned, not all of it is,' said Christobel with a wave of her hand. 'I utterly refuse to accept that there's anything revelatory about the Israelites praying for and delighting in the suffering of their enemies. The end of Psalm 137, which goes on about Babylonian babies being dashed against rocks, fills me with horror!'

'Funnily enough, those verses have been left out of the lectionary,' observed Wade dryly.

'I once thought that I'd do the right thing and read the Book of Psalms right through,' remarked Maureen. 'But all I got out of it was that the writers were paranoid about enemies and evil plots.'

'We know from Samuel that David had lots of enemies,' pointed out Frank.

Melinda nodded.

'I was told once that we should sort of understand the "enemies" as our sins,' ventured Kirsty.

'Or demons,' said Frank.

'Or the enemies of Jesus and the Church,' added Melinda. 'After all, psalms like Psalm 22 are clearly prophetic. "My God, my God, why have you forsaken me … ?"'

'Actually, the description of despair and suffering in Psalm 22 is so frightfully vivid and realish that I'm convinced that the poor writer must have been writing from personal experience,' said Christobel. 'Then Jesus, who naturally knew the psalm, drew on it to express his own feeling of being utterly abandoned by God on the cross.'

'Yes. The fact that the historical Jesus doubtless knew and may have quoted psalms does not mean that they were originally meant to be about him,' insisted Wade. 'Jews understandably resent that sort of interpretation.'

'Yet Jewish interpretations of the psalms have also changed over time,' said Ruth. 'For example: the "royal psalms" in which the king is the speaker or the focus of attention must have arisen during the monarchical period in Israelite history and been about earthly kings. However, after the monarchy disappeared they came to be thought of as referring to God's Messiah. Now it is almost impossible, when reading them as a Christian, not to think of Christ.'

'So is that why they are considered revelation?' said Kirsty, looking confused.

'What is revelation?' asked Wade airily.

'Not the Psalter dropping down from heaven and hitting King David on the head,' replied Christobel. 'You know, Kirsty, beautiful poems, like beautiful sunsets, can be frightfully evocative. They fill me with awe and I go all tingly. And the Psalter contains some of the most profound truths about God! I absolutely adore Psalm 139 (except for the horrid bits about enemies at the end which I never read):

O God, you have searched me
   and known me
You know when I sit down and
   when I rise up;
you discern my thoughts from
   far away … '

'But life isn't all beauty and joy,' declared Wade. 'Just think of all the famines, wars, and natural disasters which go on in the world. How can you reconcile them with belief in an all-powerful and all-loving God? At least the psalm writers were honest and openly accused God of failure and neglect. Yet, in spite of the fact that psalms of lament make up more than one third of the Psalter, Christians invariably remove laments from public worship and focus on praise instead. As Walter Brueggemann points out in "The Costly Loss of Lament" in *The Journal for the Study of the Old Testament* (1986), this denies the marginalized the right to voice their complaints, and sweeps hard issues of social, political, and economic justice under the carpet.'

'You mean we trot off to church and pretend to love God and be happy and thankful and all that even when it's not true?' asked Maureen. 'Well, if there's one thing I can't stand it's hypocrisy! That's why I didn't go to church for almost two months after my husband left me. How could I pray "Forgive us our trespasses as we forgive those who trespass against us"? I couldn't have forgiven him then, even if I had wanted to, which I didn't. In fact, I still don't,' she admitted honestly. 'And I wasn't just mad at *him*, either. Like Job whom we talked about last week, I was mad at God for letting it happen to me, but when I said that to the lady who came to see me to ask if I'd make half a dozen jars of jam or marmalade for the church fête, she just looked shocked and uncomfortable and left as soon as she could. And that was the only pastoral visit (if pastoral it could be called) that I got when I was going through my crisis. Oh, my best friend Enid kept popping in, but I don't count her as a church person and she wasn't much help anyway. When she wasn't suggesting that I go to Weight Watchers or have my hair tinted she was making trite remarks like "I am sure it will all turn out for the best."'

'I got really angry with God last night, too,' confided Kirsty. 'I'd prayed and prayed that Tweetie Pie would be all right … he was such a little, cute, defenceless bird, I thought God could have protected him.'

'But don't you think that the Lord of the universe has rather more important things to attend to than a budgie?' asked Melinda in a tone of gentle reproof.

'Yes, I know it was wrong to get so angry and upset,' admitted Kirsty, hanging her head.

'No it was not! It was perfectly natural,' said Christobel, reaching out to grasp Kirsty's hand. 'I am absolutely convinced that it is *vitally* important for people to be able to articulate their hurt and anger. On an individual level it is frightfully necessary if people are to develop into psychologically healthy adults and have a genuine relationship with God. I am sure that God does not want us to be outwardly saying that we love and trust her while inwardly we really dislike or fear her. However, it is also vitally important that people (especially women) who have been oppressed and ignored get together in groups to express their anger and frustration. We cannot bring about change in the Church and society if we are conditioned to accept everything as "the will of God" which we cannot question! On the other hand, when we share our stories we can empower one another and make it more likely that our voices will be heard.'

'So is there any sense in which the laments in the Psalter can be considered revelatory?' persisted Liz.

'Brueggemann believes that they are not wholly negative,' said Ruth quietly. 'On the contrary, they display "a passionate conviction that there is listening", and the hope that God will hear and act. They also characteristically move from pleas to praise, and end in thanksgiving for God's intervention. I think that it is because of this that countless Jews and Christians have found comfort and inspiration from them in times of crisis.'

'Do you think it is all right for me to think of Tweetie Pie in heaven, sort of flying around "green pastures" and "beside still waters" like it says in Psalm 23,' asked Kirsty shyly. 'I said the twenty-third Psalm this morning to myself when I was burying what was left of his poor little body.'

'I don't see why you shouldn't imagine him hopping around heaven, dear, but personally I'm sick to death of Psalm 23 at funerals,' said Maureen.

'That's a psalm of trust rather than a lament, isn't it?' said Christobel. 'Psalm 22 is definitely a lament. Rosemary Radford Ruether uses it in a rite she has developed for healing for battered wives. A group of women recite alternatively the experiences of a battered woman and verses from the psalm.'

'You found that in Holladay's *The Psalms Through Three Thousand Years: Prayerbook of a Cloud of Witnesses*, didn't you?' said Wade. 'Holladay also quotes the paraphrase that Nicaraguan poet Ernesto Cardenal has made of Psalm 22 in the light of political persecution in South America:

Lord O Lord my God
why have you left me?
I am a caricature of a man
People think that I am dirt

they mock me in all the papers
I am encircled
there are tanks all round me
Machine-gunners have me in their sights
there is barbed wire about me
electrified wire
I am on a list
I am called all day
They have tattooed me
and marked me with a number ...
Yet
I shall tell my brothers and sisters
about you
I shall praise you in our nation
and my hymns will be heard
in a great generation
The poor will go to a banquet
and our people will give a great feast
the new people
yet to be born.'

'I suppose the fact that the psalm writers don't specify the exact nature of their suffering, or their particular enemies, means that people throughout history have been able to read the psalms in the light of their own situations,' reflected Ruth. 'They really do have a timeless quality about them.'

'Yes, I am sure that the Book of Psalms will still be being read long after the latest trendy theologies are forgotten,' said Melinda curtly.

'But we shouldn't go tampering with the Word of God,' maintained Frank, thumping his Bible. 'It's not for us to change what God said, like Cardenal did, or add bits about women being battered.'

'Haven't you realized yet that you only have a translation of the Bible, you do not have a copy of God's actual words?' said Wade with an exasperated sigh. 'Different versions of the Hebrew text survive, and even the best manuscripts sometimes betray evidence of omissions, alterations, and additions. Then, when the best possible Hebrew text is translated into English, a literal translation doesn't always make sense. Some words and phrases are virtually untranslatable, and we miss an enormous amount of the poetic word-plays, alliterations, rhythms, and so on, that would have been apparent in the original.'

'I know that when we are studying the Bible we need to use a translation that is as close to the original as possible,' said Ruth, 'but surely when we use the Bible for devotional purposes what matters most is that the translation helps us communicate with God?'

'And for an increasing number of women, androcentric language and imagery is a huge turn-off,' declared Christobel, 'which is why I like the way the Carmelite Order in the United States has used inclusive language in its adaptation of the Liturgy of the Hours. Instead of "The Lord is my shepherd,/ I shall not want./He makes me lie down", etc., God is addressed in the second person: "Yahweh, you are my shepherd,/I shall not want./You make me to lie in green pastures … "'

'Of course, the words in the middle of the twenty-third Psalm have always been in the second person,' mused Ruth, '"Even though I walk through the valley of the shadow of death, I will fear no evil, for you are with me". In the rest of the Bible we read about God, and what God said through the prophets, and what people remembered that Jesus had said, and what Paul wrote, and so on, but when the psalms move into the first and second persons we can actually begin to talk to God ourselves, and we can sense God's response in the words of the psalm: "Do not be afraid. I am your shepherd, I will protect you." And the amazing thing is, no matter what one's situation, happy or sad, rejoicing in victory or dreadfully depressed, full of life or in great pain, there will be a verse somewhere in the Psalter that one can relate to.'

'Is there anything about ex-husbands?' asked Maureen hopefully.

'Psalm 55 certainly speaks of the pain of being betrayed by your closest friend,' Ruth answered. 'And I'm sure that there are others that you would find helpful too.'

'Here's one for Tweetie Pie,' contributed Jason, who had been flicking through his Bible. 'Psalm 50: "I know all the birds of the air, and all that moves in the field is mine," says God. And in Psalm 57 there's talk about sheltering under God's wings (Tweetie Pie would be able to relate to God as a mother bird), and being saved from lions (I suppose a cat would be like a lion to a budgie), and singing and making melodies and awakening the dawn. I can just see Tweetie Pie up in heaven, driving all the souls who want to sleep nuts.'

Kirsty looked somewhat comforted.

'Ruth, I am glad that you raised the subject of prayer because the Psalter has been described as a "school of prayer",' said Liz. 'So one final question, what do you think that we can learn about prayer from it?'

She looked around the room.

'That God is always listening,' suggested Kirsty.

'That it is all right to be honest with God,' declared Maureen, 'and thank God for that!'

'That we should "be still and know that [the Lord is] God", like it says in Psalm 46,' said Melinda.

'That there are times for laments, just as there are times for celebrations,' cried Christobel. 'And our celebration liturgies should be more dramatic, with singing and dancing and trumpets and tambourines and loud, clashing cymbals like it says in Psalm 150!'

Christobel didn't have a trumpet or tambourine on hand, all she could do was jump up and down and exuberantly clap her hands. Dave, whose head had been sinking lower and lower onto his chest, woke with a start. 'Oh, good grief, is that the time? I must get going. I've got an appointment with my physiotherapist.'

'We'll all finish up,' said Liz. 'But before you go, I hope that we can all agree that the psalms can be a great help in both our private devotions and our public worship. And with regard to the latter, although laments and dramatic liturgies might not be as common today as they were in ancient Israel, we should never underestimate the significance of the Psalter in shaping Jewish and Christian worship. From the Second Temple period after the exile, when the psalms were collected and arranged in their present form, the Psalter has been seen as reflecting in a very special way the community's experience of its relationship with God, and it has been the medium through which generation after generation has come to share in that experience.'

'Psalm 145 verse 4: "One generation shall laud your works to another, and shall declare your mighty acts",' quoted Frank.

'Mmm,' said Maureen reflectively. 'Perhaps I'll tell my kids I want Psalm 100 at my funeral. At least it's cheerful and short … '

WEEK·NINE

Proverbs and Ecclesiastes

Today we had to discuss two of the books in the Old Testament which are classified as 'wisdom literature' – Proverbs and Ecclesiastes. When everyone had arrived except Dave, Liz started the ball rolling by asking where Israelite wisdom literature had come from?

'Solomon, of course,' said Frank. 'It says so at the beginning of Proverbs: "The proverbs of Solomon, son of David, king of Israel".'

'Then, in chapter 22, it says "the words of the wise",' interrupted Wade, 'and in chapter 24, "these are also sayings of the wise". Likewise, in chapter 30, we are told that these are "the words of Agur son of Jakeh", and finally, in chapter 31: "the words of King Lemuel. An oracle that his mother taught him". You refuse to accept that the Pentateuch has been put together from different sources, but you *have* to acknowledge that more than one writer contributed to Proverbs!'

'Yes, it is clearly an anthology of proverbs,' said Melinda calmly, 'but Solomon probably wrote most of them and compiled the rest. We know from 1 Kings that when God asked Solomon what he wanted, instead of saying wealth or long life, Solomon opted for understanding to discern what was right. God was so pleased with that answer that he promised Solomon riches and honour as well.'

'"God gave Solomon very great wisdom, discernment, and breadth of understanding as vast as the sand on the seashore",' read Frank from 1 Kings 4, '"so that Solomon's wisdom surpassed the wisdom of all the people of Egypt. He was wiser than anyone else, wiser than Ethan the Ezrahite [whoever he was] … his fame spread throughout the surrounding nations … " That's true, you know, because even the Queen of Sheba came to visit him, and she couldn't get over how wise he was.'

'I wonder if they had an affair?' mused Maureen. 'You wouldn't have thought he would have had time, what with his seven hundred wives and three hundred concubines, but I wouldn't put anything past him. Dirty old devil.'

'The legend of Solomon's great wisdom meant that people attributed wisdom literature to him to give it extra clout,' said Wade in an exasperated tone, 'just like psalms were attributed to David and the Pentateuch to Moses.'

Frank muttered something incoherent.

'Well, who were "the wise", Agur, Lemuel, and Lemuel's mum?' asked Maureen.

'No one knows,' answered Wade, 'but Agur, Lemuel, and his mum were probably not Israelites, and the "words of the wise" have clearly been adapted from an ancient Egyptian text, *Instructions of Amenemope*.'

'Rubbish,' snorted Frank.

'Why?' demanded Wade. 'You said just now that his fame spread, and people like the Queen of Sheba visited him to see what he had to say. Doesn't that indicate that interest in wisdom crossed national borders? It was an international movement, not one confined to Israel.'

'A certain amount of wisdom is common human wisdom which can be shared by different societies,' conceded Melinda.

'Yes,' said Liz, 'but who do you think among the Israelites could have been responsible for adapting and compiling wisdom traditions, if not Solomon?'

'Obviously scribes and officials at the royal court,' replied Wade, before anyone else could speak. 'There is evidence of that in chapter 25: "These are other proverbs of Solomon that the officials of King Hezekiah of Judah copied ... " There must have been a professional class of wise men at court, men trained in writing and diplomacy, who reflected on what was the proper role of the king, how they should behave at court, and so on:

> Do not put yourself forward in the king's presence
> or stand in the place of the great;
> for it is better to be told, "Come up here,"
> than to be put lower in the presence of a noble. (25:6–7)'

'Here's another one,' said Maureen with a pleased expression. '"When you sit down to eat with a ruler, observe carefully what is before you, and put a knife to your throat if you have a big appetite." Sounds a bit drastic, but I expect it's a warning not to be greedy. Before I took my kids out anywhere where there'd be food, I'd always try to fill them up at home so they wouldn't make pigs of themselves.'

'The proverbs aren't all about kings and courtiers, are they?' said Ruth. 'Many seem to be advice from parents to a child: "Hear, my child, your father's instruction, and do not neglect your mother's teaching ... "'

'I'm glad that mothers get a mention for once,' declared Maureen. 'Where did I see ... ? Oh yes, 15:20, "the foolish despise their mother". I must remember to tell Neil that the next time he gets fed up with me telling him that he should wear warm underwear. In the middle of winter he'll go out wearing just jeans, a T-shirt and a light jacket, and then wonder why he keeps getting colds! Oh, and here's another one: "Foolish children are a grief to their father and bitterness to her who bore them." Well, the author got that around the wrong way. It's mothers who are grieved and fathers who are bitter when their sons don't turn out the way they want and blame their wives for not bringing them up properly, but if Don had spent more time at home with his kids and less at the golf club! I was left to do all the child raising, and it's no good telling me "those who spare the rod hate their children, but those who love them are diligent to discipline them". I could never catch the little blighter to give him a whack … '

'Thank you, Ruth and Maureen, for raising the family "flavour" which characterizes many of the proverbs,' said Liz quickly. 'Some scholars believe that they reflect family or folk wisdom, which was passed on down the generations in society as a whole, rather than in the élite environment of the royal court. However, while theories abound, I am afraid that there is very little concrete evidence about the dates and original life settings of the proverbs. Probably the book reflects a mixture of family and court wisdom, from different authors and different periods. Can we put the historical issues aside now and try to define what a proverb actually is?'

'I read somewhere that it is a short saying,' ventured Kirsty, 'which sort of embodies a truth gleaned from experience or observation, and it is expressed in a poetic form to make it easy to remember.'

Liz said that that was a very good definition.

'Isn't there some lovely poetic imagery?' commented Ruth. 'One of my favourites is:

Like cold water to a thirsty soul,
so is good news from a far country. (25:25)'

135

'That's an example of synthetic or progressive parallelism,' expounded Wade. 'The second line builds on the first. Parallelism is, of course, the most common poetic form in Proverbs. Another variation is antithetic parallelism which juxtaposes two opposites, as in:

> The memory of the righteous is a blessing,
> but the name of the wicked will rot. (10:7)

'And occasionally there is synonymous parallelism, which reinforces an observation by making the same point in a slightly different way:

> My child, be attentive to my words;
> incline your ear to my sayings. (4:20)'

'My old mother was a great one for quoting proverbs,' recalled Maureen. '"You can lead a horse to water but you can't make it drink," "A rolling stone gathers no moss," "All that glitters is not gold," and so on. They're not in the Bible, are they? No, I didn't think so. But this one is, I found it last night, and it was one of Mother's favourites: "Do not boast about tomorrow, for you do not know what a day may bring." She'd often say that, and "Let your foot be seldom in your neighbour's house, otherwise your neighbour will become weary of you and hate you." I never realized how true that was until some years ago a family moved into the house next door, and the kids were about the same age as mine, so naturally they played together, and I got to know Elaine, the mother. At first it was real nice having someone in the street my own age whom I could talk to, but she kept popping in when it wasn't convenient, and she'd borrow things and never bring them back, and she'd gossip endlessly. The things I heard about some of the other people in the street! I must admit, that was quite an enjoyable aspect of our friendship at first, but one day my neighbour on the other side said something which made me realize that she knew something about me and Don which I'd told Elaine in confidence. I began to wonder what else she'd been saying about me behind my back. Eventually I tackled her about that, and she turned real nasty and said some horrible spiteful things. It wasn't pleasant, I can tell you! And we had to go on living next door to one another, trying to ignore each other when we were out in our back gardens hanging out the washing ... '

'There are quite a few proverbs about the harm that gossip and hot-tempered words can do,' observed Ruth.

'And there are lots about nasty wives,' added Jason with a grin. '"It is better to live in a corner of the housetop than in a house shared with a contentious wife"!'

'Houses in ancient Israel had flat roofs,' commented Wade. 'A modern paraphrase would be: "It is better to live in a garage than in a house with a contentious wife".'

'In any case, that clearly shows that the proverbs were written from a male perspective,' Christobel spat out. 'There's none about it being better to live in the corner of a housetop than with a violent, abusive, drunken husband!'

'Not specifically, perhaps,' said Melinda, 'but drunkenness is condemned:

Who has woe? Who has sorrow?
Who has strife? Who has complaining?
Who has wounds without cause?
Who has redness of eyes?
Those who linger late over wine ... '

'That might be so, but most proverbs are still frightfully male-centred,' continued Christobel hotly. 'There are all those tirades about how men should avoid loose women and adulteresses, but nothing about how they should not seduce innocent virgins! The woman is always portrayed as the temptress, never the victim.'

'Well, in my opinion (and believe me, I can speak from experience), both a woman and a man are to blame if they have an adulterous affair,' declared Maureen. 'It takes two to tango, as Mother used to say. But, in any case, it says in Proverbs 5 that a man should stick to the wife of his youth, and so he should.'

'Not scattering his streams in the streets,' said Jason, reading Proverbs 5:16.

'I suppose that refers to sex,' said Maureen bluntly. 'I don't always understand the cryptic stuff. The ant one makes sense, though: "Go to the ant, you lazybones: consider its ways and be wise … "'

'Yeah, laziness gets about as good a press in Proverbs as adultery, gossip, and drunkenness,' continued Jason. 'Whoever wrote them must have been real killjoys.'

'"Folly is a joy to one who has no sense",' quoted Melinda with a cold glance in Jason's direction.

Jason hunted through his Bible for a suitable rejoinder.

'Come to think of it, all that stuff about a man being faithful to his wife couldn't have been written by Solomon,' reflected Maureen, 'unless he had real cheek.'

'Yes, someone with over a thousand women in his harem shouldn't give other men lectures on fidelity,' agreed Jason, looking up from his Bible. 'It's not fair.'

'I am proud to say … ' began Melinda.

'"Pride goes before destruction, and a haughty spirit before a fall,"' Jason got in gleefully.

'As Kirsty said earlier,' intervened Liz, 'the proverbs are obviously *human* observations or reflections on *human* experience. God rarely gets a mention. So why is this book in the Bible? How did it come to be considered in some way revelation?'

'Solomon was inspired by God to show us how God wants us to live our lives,' maintained Frank.

'"If you have found honey, eat only enough for you, or else, having too much, you will vomit it,"' quoted Jason. 'Hey, thanks for the tip, God.'

'Mars bars are my downfall,' remarked Maureen. 'I can never resist eating just a bit more than I should and then I end up feeling sick.'

'I can just see it,' said Jason in a rapt voice, 'the heavens open, choirs of angels appear, bopping away with their harps, and then there is an ear-splitting drum roll. A voice booms down: "DO NOT EAT TOO MANY MARS BARS OR ELSE YOU'LL THROW UP!"'

Christobel giggled.

'That's not how revelation occurs,' said Melinda sharply.

'How does it then?' asked Jason.

'The Holy Spirit *gently* guided Solomon's thoughts ... ' began Melinda.

'So that he came up with profound things like "The clever do all things intelligently, but the fool displays folly,"' scoffed Wade.

'The great range of subject matter and the varying degrees of profundity in the Book of Proverbs show how interested God is in all aspects of human life and how he wants to relate to people of varying degrees of intelligence,' said Melinda resolutely.

'And a proverb which appears simple at first can become more profound the more you think about it,' said Ruth. 'The one you mentioned, Jason, about not eating too much honey could apply to things other than sweet food. Anything pleasant and appealing can become unpleasant if you have a surfeit of it.'

'Which is plain common sense,' concluded Wade, 'so where does God come in?'

'It was God who gave us common sense,' insisted Melinda, 'and the ability to reason, reflect, and observe, and the desire to seek knowledge. Unfortunately, however, because of all the sin and rebellion in the world, many people seek knowledge apart from God. They think that they can become wise through their own efforts, without bothering about God. The fundamental message of the Book of Proverbs, the key to understanding it, is spelled out in Proverbs 1:7: "the fear of the Lord is the beginning of knowledge". Only those in a right relationship with God can attain a true understanding of reality.'

Wade gave a contemptuous snort. 'You might have a high opinion of the theology of Proverbs, but I'm afraid I don't. As Crenshaw says in his *Old Testament Wisdom: An Introduction*, the wisdom writers were trying to "ferret out" the secrets of the universe so that they could live in harmony with the world order, and as a result be blessed with long life, children, wealth, prosperity, etc. I suppose that it was a religious quest in so far as the secrets were thought to have been planted there by God, but the end result is a reward/retribution theology which equates wisdom with righteousness and blessing, and folly with wickedness and punishment:

The Lord does not let the righteous go hungry,
but he thwarts the cravings of the wicked. (10:3)

The fear of the Lord prolongs life,
but the years of the wicked will be short. (10:27)

The perverse get what their ways deserve,
and the good, what their deeds deserve. (14:14)

'That's exactly the sort of theology the author of Job was combating!'

'And I think it's absolutely appalling,' exclaimed Christobel.

'And, as well as being written from a male perspective,' continued Wade, 'the proverbs are also written from a well-to-do middle-class perspective. There is no real understanding of the plight of the poor and no concern for social reform: the existence of poverty is simply taken for granted. At best the middle-class hearers of the proverbs are exhorted to be charitable to poor people because this will benefit *them*: "Whoever is kind to the poor lends to the Lord, and will be repaid in full." However, the overall message is that poverty is the result of folly and laziness, so work hard to make sure it doesn't befall you!'

'Yet wisdom is seen as far more important than wealth,' argued Melinda. '"For wisdom is better than jewels, and all that you desire cannot compare with her" (8:11).'

'Ah, but read a few verses down,' said Wade, '"Riches and honour are with me, enduring wealth and prosperity." The point is that wisdom will enable you to get long-lasting wealth!'

'Yes, but isn't there still recognition that wealth is not everything?' said Ruth, coming down on Melinda's side. 'What about …

Better is little with fear of the Lord
than great wealth and trouble with it.
Better is a dinner of vegetables where love is
than a fatted ox and hatred with it. (15:16–17)

Better is a little with righteousness
than large income with injustice. (16:8)

A good name is to be chosen rather than great riches. (22:1)'

'"Riches do not profit in the day of wrath, but righteousness delivers from death,"' added Melinda grimly.

'And "Those who trust in their riches will wither, but the righteous will flourish like green leaves,"' said Frank triumphantly.

'Ha! Ha! You're all wrong!' cried Jason, turning to the Book of Ecclesiastes. 'Wealth, wisdom, righteousness ... it's all meaningless, meaningless, vanity, vanity ... It doesn't matter whether you're wealthy or poor, wise or a fool, pious or impious, sooner or later you'll still end up dead and that's the end!'

'Which represents a totally different view from those of the authors of Proverbs,' said Wade, leaning forward eagerly. 'Whereas the latter were intent on seeking wisdom, long life and prosperity, Qoheleth concludes that searching for wisdom is "chasing after wind". No matter how hard you toil calamities can befall you, and you'd have been better off if you'd never been born. All you can do is enjoy what you can while you can.'

'Who's Qoheleth?' asked Maureen.

'The author of Ecclesiastes introduces himself as "Qoheleth",' explained Liz. 'It's a Hebrew word sometimes translated as "Teacher", but it comes from a root that means to assemble or gather, so it could imply that he was a gatherer of wisdom sayings. The word "Ecclesiastes" comes from the Greek *ecclesia* which means a gathering.'

'But the author goes on to say that he was the son of David, king in Jerusalem,' said Frank, 'so obviously he must have been Solomon.'

'That's another literary fiction,' sighed Wade. 'Elsewhere he refers to all the kings who preceded him in Jerusalem (if he really was Solomon, there was only David) and he clearly writes as a subject not a king. The language he uses is late Hebrew, more characteristic of the third or second century

BCE than the tenth ... '

'Well, one thing is certain about whoever wrote it,' said Maureen. 'He sure was depressed! I know just how he must have felt. When Don left me I got real depressed, too. I couldn't sleep properly, or eat properly, or make any decisions. Everything seemed hopeless. I just moped around the house all day doing nothing. Eventually my kids got fed up and made me go to see a psychiatrist. I didn't want to take drugs, but he reckoned that the latest anti-depressants don't have the bad side effects that older ones used to, so I gave in, and the tablets sure helped a lot. I realized that I wasn't going nuts, it was just that I had this chemical imbalance in my body, and I wasn't the only one. Depression is so common ....'

'Because we live in such a sick society,' declared Frank with a zealous gleam in his eyes. 'It's not drugs that people need but Jesus! That's the whole point of Ecclesiastes. Solomon wrote it late in his life after he'd rebelled against God. God inspired him to write about the despair of an unsaved man. But we know that Jesus redeems us from death and restores meaning to our lives. Praise the Lord!'

'And what does Melinda think?' asked Wade, crossing his arms.

'I accept that it was not necessarily written by Solomon,' replied Melinda. 'Two men must have contributed to it. One was very sceptical, but the other was an orthodox wisdom teacher who wrote the prologue and chapter 12. He was plainly trying to highlight the dangers of speculative, doubting wisdom (so like much modern scholarship) to his students. His positive teaching is contained in 12:13–14 where he calls students back to a right relationship with God: "The end of the matter: all has been heard. Fear God and keep his commandments; for that is the whole duty of everyone. For

God will bring every deed into judgement, including every secret thing, whether good or evil."'

'That's a typical example of the way defenders of orthodoxy have edited radical texts to make them more acceptable,' said Wade, looking annoyed.

'It might make it a *bit* more acceptable, but Ecclesiastes still seems an odd book to find in the Bible to me,' said Maureen.

'Yeah! Fancy part of the Bible being written by an atheist!' exclaimed Jason.

'Oh, I don't think that the author was that radical,' said Ruth. 'He still believed in God, he just found God distant and not to be trusted. Sadly, that is still the experience of people today. If I'm honest, I have to admit that there are times in my life when God seems far away too.'

'It's perfectly natural,' agreed Christobel, 'but not really true. The fabulous thing about Proverbs is the way it shows how Sophia *wants* to be found, how she goes into the market places preaching, and invites people to her banquet, and how she passionately promotes justice … '

'Sophia? Do you mean Wisdom?' asked Kirsty.

'*Sophia* is the Greek word for wisdom,' said Liz, 'which is personified as a woman in parts of Proverbs.'

'The personification is, however, purely poetic,' explained Melinda, 'like some people talk about "Mother Nature" or "Mother Church". It is naturally not meant to imply that Lady Wisdom is a divine being.'

'But,' cried Christobel, 'Sophia says in Proverbs 8:

The Lord created me at the beginning of his work,
    the first of his acts of long ago.
Ages ago I was set up, at the first, before the
    beginning of the earth …

When he established the heavens, I was there,
　when he drew a circle on the face of the deep,
when he made firm the skies above,
　when he established the fountains of the deep,
when he assigned to the sea its limit,
　so that the waters might not transgress his command,
when he marked out the foundations of the earth,
　then I was beside him, like a master worker;
and I was daily his delight,
　rejoicing before him always,
rejoicing in his inhabited world
　and delighting in the human race.'

'Yes, Sophia is presented as God's companion or spouse,' remarked Wade, 'which doubtless represents the remnants of goddess worship in Israel.'

'Corrupted though some Israelites became by pagan cults, I hardly think that orthodox Israelites would have countenanced the references to Lady Wisdom in Proverbs if that was the case,' said Melinda. 'It is totally contrary to Israel's belief in *one* God alone.'

'Yet Sophia seems to have characteristics of God,' said Ruth quietly. 'That comes out most clearly in the Wisdom of Solomon, where she is described as holy, all-knowing, all-powerful, and everywhere present:

For she is a breath of the power of God,
and a pure emanation of the glory of the Almighty;
therefore nothing defiled gains entrance into her.
For she is a reflection of eternal light,
a spotless mirror of the working of God,
and an image of his goodness.
Although she is but one, she can do all things,

and while remaining in herself, she renews all things;
in every generation she passes into holy souls
and makes them friends of God and prophets;
for God loves nothing so much
as the person who lives with wisdom. (7:25–28)

'Then, not only is she credited with creating and sustaining all things, but also with *saving* humans. It says in chapter 10 that she protected Adam and delivered him from his sin, and rescued Noah and his family from the Flood and Lot from the destruction of Sodom. She also helped Jacob and Joseph during their trials, and last but not least, delivered the Israelites from oppression in Egypt!

She entered the soul of a servant of the Lord,
and withstood dread kings with wonders and signs.
She gave to holy people the rewards of their labours;
she guided them along a marvellous way,
and became a shelter to them by day,
and a starry flame through the night.
She brought them over the Red Sea,
and led them through deep waters … '

'So what do you conclude from that, Ruth?' asked Liz.

'That Sophia is not another God but God as God relates to the world, God's way of revealing God's self and communicating with human beings.'

'I absolutely agree,' exclaimed Christobel. 'Sophia is a simply marvellous way of imaging the divine as a female figure.'

'What's this Wisdom of Solomon,' muttered Frank. 'I've never heard of it before.'

'It is part of the Apocrypha, which is accepted as canonical by Catholic and Orthodox churches,' said Liz, 'however, during the Reformation Protestants adopted a shorter canon and left it out. The Anglicans tried to keep a foot in both camps, retaining the Apocrypha as "an example of life and instruction of manner" but not "to establish any doctrine", as it says in the Thirty-Nine Articles.'

'The author of the Wisdom of Solomon was probably a Jew living in Alexandria in the first century BCE,' expounded Wade. 'He wrote in Greek, and was heavily influenced by Greek culture as well as Jewish religious traditions. His personification of wisdom as a female could well have been designed to provide Jews attracted to the worship of the Egyptian goddess Isis with an acceptable alternative.'

'Did a Solomon really write it, or was it just called the Wisdom of Solomon so that people would think King Solomon wrote it?' asked Kirsty.

'The latter,' replied Wade.

'Isn't that sort of dishonest?' said Kirsty.

'Yeah, which is why it isn't in proper Bibles,' declared Frank. 'And it was written so many years after Solomon died, that it can't possibly contain his inspired teaching.'

'Where does that leave Proverbs and Ecclesiastes, then?' said Jason. 'Much the same could be said about them.'

'The Wisdom of Solomon might have been written long after Solomon, but it was written very close to the time of Jesus,' pointed out Ruth. 'What I find fascinating is the way some of the early Christians came to understand Jesus as Sophia, the Wisdom of God, in human form. Hebrews 1:3 speaks of Jesus in just about the same language as the Wisdom of Solomon speaks of Sophia: "He is the reflection of God's glory and exact imprint of God's very being, and he sustains all things by his powerful word ... " Colossians also contains wisdom overtones: "He is the image of the invisible God, the firstborn of all creation; for in him all things in heaven and on earth were created, things visible and invisible … "'

'And Jesus went around the streets talking to people, and eating with them like the Wisdom woman does in Proverbs, and telling parables and other wise things,' said Maureen, 'so I reckon you're onto something there, Ruth.'

'It does help explain the doctrines of the Incarnation and the Trinity,' said Ruth, 'how we can say that Jesus Christ was born a baby in Bethlehem at a particular time in history, yet was present at the creation of the world, and has such a close relationship with God that we can identify him with God.'

'Jesus is certainly the Wisdom of God, but we mustn't read too much into the personification of wisdom in Proverbs,' warned Melinda. 'After all, folly is personified as a woman too.'

'Well, Proverbs was probably written or put together by men,' said Christobel, 'so you can't expect too much. It's a miracle that there is at least one positive presentation of a female figure!'

'There's also that model wife right at the end, in chapter 31,' added Maureen. 'The one who gets up while it is still dark and works her fingers to the bone for her family.'

'I think that that is a very good way of ending Proverbs,' said Melinda. 'The book begins by inviting young men to fall in love with Lady Wisdom, and it ends by advising them to appreciate a wise wife "far more precious than jewels" who will help them attain the wealth, honour, happiness, and long life which result from following wisdom.'

'Well, I think it's sickening,' said Christobel frankly. 'The woman is solely seen as a wife and mother, not a person in her own right, and she sets impossibly high standards for other women to follow.'

'I read that it is an acrostic poem,' remarked Ruth. 'We can't tell that in English, but apparently in Hebrew every line begins with a successive letter of the Hebrew alphabet.'

'So the author could have put some bits in because he couldn't think of any thing else that fitted,' said Maureen.

'Yes, but it is very cleverly done,' acknowledged Liz. 'It makes a point about the benefits that can arise from a combination of wisdom and hard work. However, don't forget that wisdom literature like this is poetry, and poetry is not always meant to be taken literally. We surely don't all have to get up before dawn because that is what the woman is supposed to have done in 31:15.'

'So how do we use Proverbs and Ecclesiastes today?' asked Maureen.

'I think there are some real gems of wisdom in both books,' said Ruth thoughtfully, 'but we need to be wise in the way we use them. We can't just make a rash decision, then commit it to the Lord like it says in 16:3, and expect that our plan will automatically succeed because God promised it would. Proverbs don't work that way. They are so brief that they only state a general truth, what is *likely* to happen if you follow a certain course. There will always be exceptions, partly because we live in an imperfect world, and no matter how hard we try, our understanding of it is always going to be inadequate. Also, God cannot be pinned down or manipulated:

> No wisdom, no understanding, no counsel,
> can avail against the Lord.
> The horse is made ready for the day of battle,
> but the victory belongs to the Lord.'

'It sure is confusing at times,' said Maureen. 'You've got to know when it's appropriate to say "Moderation in all things," and when "You can never get too much of a good thing."'

'"Look before you leap" or "He who hesitates is lost"?' added Wade with a smile.

'That is why it is so important that we consider the whole body of inspired teaching,' stressed Melinda. 'The way to approach wisdom literature is to study it prayerfully, with the aim of becoming more *mature* and better equipped to live the way that God wants us to, not to pluck verses out of context in the hope that they will provide instant answers to whatever problems are besetting us at the moment!'

Liz agreed.

WEEK·TEN

The Song of Songs

No Jason or Dave today. Liz revealed that Dave was in hospital. He had been in a nasty collision with another player in his soccer match, and ended up with a depressed fracture of the right cheekbone, a broken jaw, and two nose fractures. Jason had also sent his apologies, but the only thing wrong with him was a cold. I suppose I shouldn't say 'only' – a cold can be very unpleasant, it just doesn't seem as dramatic as Dave's injuries. Kirsty offered to send Dave a card on behalf of us all, and Maureen said that she would make Jason some of her special lemon cordial, which her kids really loved when they had colds.

After Christobel and Maureen had made arrangements for Christobel to pick up the cordial and deliver it to Jason, we got started on the Song of Songs. I've never really known what to make of the Song. Always put it in the 'too hard' basket. Liz, however, said that it is part of the Megilloth.

'Megawhat?' interrupted Maureen.

'The five scrolls in the Hebrew Bible,' explained Liz, 'which we know as Song of Songs, Ruth, Lamentations, Ecclesiastes, and Esther. They're scattered throughout our Bibles, but in the Hebrew Bible they belong together, and from at least the early medieval period they have been read at Israel's annual acts of worship: the Song of Songs at Passover,

Ruth at Pentecost, Lamentations on the Ninth of Ab, Ecclesiastes at Tabernacles, and Esther at Purim. So would anyone like to hazard a guess as to when the Song of Songs was composed?'

'You don't have to guess,' said Frank. 'It was written in the tenth century by Solomon. It says so at the beginning.'

'No one takes the ascription to Solomon seriously today,' said Wade scornfully. 'It was written long after he was dead. But if you're going to base your argument on the first line, you might as well know that Marcia Falk says in the notes to her translation in *Love Lyrics from the Bible* that it could literally be translated "the song of songs which is by, *or* to, *or* of, *or* about Solomon", so it cannot be assumed to indicate the author.'

'I don't see why Solomon could not have been the author,' retorted Melinda. 'After all, 1 Kings 4:32 says that he composed 3000 proverbs and 1005 songs ... '

'And he must've been obsessed with sex, if the number in his harem is anything to go by,' contributed Maureen.

'What is more,' continued Melinda, resolutely ignoring this less reputable aspect of Solomon's character, 'there is a reference in 6:4 to the city of Tirzah, which scholars believe could only have been made before Samaria replaced Tirzah as the capital of the northern kingdom *c.*870 BC, and probably even before the division of the kingdom after Solomon's death.'

'That is one argument,' agreed Liz, 'but other scholars find evidence of Persian and Greek words and conclude that the Song must therefore have been written after the exile.'

'Couldn't the fact that the Song seems to reflect an age of worldliness and luxury indicate that it may have come from Solomon's time?' asked Ruth. 'There do not seem to be any hints of the later crises that the Israelites experienced.'

'But that could simply be the result of the common tendency to look back on an almost forgotten past as a "golden age", as in the legends of King Arthur,' argued Wade.

'Yes, I'm afraid that nothing is known for sure about the date of composition,' said Liz. 'Suggestions have ranged from the tenth century to the third BCE. And nothing for certain is known about the author or editor, either. There is disagreement among scholars as to whether the Song is one great song (*the* song of songs) or an anthology of smaller songs (the song of *songs*). I think that the majority of scholars are now inclined to accept the latter view. However, that raises the issue of whether the editor basically just did a "cut and paste" job, putting together a number of poems which could have come from different poets living in different periods, or whether he (or she) had a much more active and creative role in shaping the final version.'

'But the Song of Songs is definitely about Solomon, isn't it?' asked Kirsty in a small voice. 'I mean, there's that bit at the beginning when the woman says that the king has brought her into his chamber, and then there's the description of Solomon's wedding procession in chapter 3 ... '

'Did you come across any of the explanations that have been put forward to account for the royal imagery?' asked Liz.

'Some of the songs could originally have come from a cult, such as the Tammuz-Ishtar cult,' responded Wade coolly. 'Tammuz and Ishtar were the Babylonian dying and rising gods who were associated with fertility, and sacred marriage ceremonies were held between their earthly representatives, a king and a priestess, to ensure prosperity each year. Songs were composed to stimulate sexual desire in those who heard them, and thus contribute to the growth and well being of society.'

Melinda wrinkled up her nose disdainfully.

'I hardly think that the Songs of Songs would have got into the canon of Sacred Scripture if that was its original purpose,' she stated.

'But by the time it was canonized the original purpose could have been forgotten,' maintained Wade.

'And if the Deuterowhatnot historian and the prophets are to be believed, the Israelites were forever backsliding into goodness knows what sort of Canaanite religious practices,' said Maureen with a nod, 'so it wouldn't surprise me at all if some of them got carried over. Happens all the time. Wasn't Christmas Day originally the birthday of some pagan god or other before the early Christians decided to make it Jesus' birthday?'

Frank said that the issue of the origins of December 25 as Christmas Day (which isn't mentioned in the Bible) is entirely different from that of the Song of Songs, as the Song *is* in the Bible, and therefore God wrote it through Solomon.

Wade raised his eyes skyward.

'Any more theories about the type of writing, origins or original purpose of the Song?' asked Liz with a rather desperate sort of cheerfulness.

'Wasn't the drama theory especially popular in the nineteenth century?' said Ruth. 'There seem to have been two main versions: one in which the two major characters were thought to be a shepherd and a young woman; and the other in which Solomon was the villain who sought to entice the young woman away from her humble lover, but true love won out in the end.'

'Sounds more like a melodrama or a farce to me,' said Maureen. 'Actually, I might just be dumb, but I can't make any sense of the Song of Songs at all. Half the time you don't know whether the woman is dreaming or not ... '

'It is interesting that you should say that, Maureen,' said

Liz encouragingly, 'because, according to another theory, the whole thing *is* a dream, and as I'm sure we all know from personal experience, dreams usually lack order and logic.'

This prompted Maureen to reveal that she dreamed last night that she tried to chop her ex-husband up and put him in the blender.

'What a horrible nightmare!' exclaimed Kirsty.

'It wasn't really, just frustrating. He wouldn't keep still.'

'You poor darling,' cried Christobel. 'You know what this means, of course. You are unconsciously suppressing your anger. Have you ever considered going to anger release sessions? I have a friend who's found it amazingly therapeutic to hit a punch bag.'

Maureen said that she thought that it would be a waste of time and energy hitting a bag, and Ruth confided that she has learnt that whenever she goes on a shopping spree it usually means that deep down she is angry about something. I suppose that when you're a nun who's taken a vow of poverty, buying things is a pretty rebellious sort of thing to do.

'I always try to go for a long walk when I'm mad,' said Liz, 'but anyway, getting back to the Song, so far we've got the cultic theory, the dramatic theory, and the dream theory. Any others?'

'It could have been a collection of songs used in wedding celebrations,' declared Wade. 'That would in part explain the royal imagery: the groom was called "king" (although there is no reference to the bride being called "queen", which rather mucks the theory up). However, a feature of Syrian wedding festivities even in recent times has been a descriptive poem or "wasf" which praises the beauty of the bride and groom. There are clear examples of "wasfs" in 4:1–7, 5:10–16 and 7:1–6.'

'Are those the parts where the man says that the woman's eyes are like doves, and all that?' asked Kirsty.

'And her hair is like a flock of goats, and her teeth like shorn ewes,' added Maureen. 'I'd hardly call them compliments, and being told that you have a nose like a tower of Lebanon overlooking Damascus is downright insulting. My ex-husband never used to say nice things about me, but I have to admit that he came closer to the truth saying that my breasts were like poached eggs than two fawns. Why on earth would someone say that his girlfriend's breasts were like deer? Didn't she have a bra? Did they bounce around a lot?'

'The imagery in the Song of Songs does seem frightfully strange to us,' admitted Christobel, 'but it's amazing the way people see beauty differently in different cultures. Just think of those poor women in Africa who try to make their necks really long.'

'Crenshaw says in *Old Testament, Story and Faith: A Literary and Theological Introduction* that when the poet describes the woman's hair as "like a flock of goats", he really means that it is wavy,' commented Ruth rather doubtfully. 'Likewise, her teeth sparkled "like shorn ewes", and her nose was graceful "like a tower in Lebanon".'

Maureen was unconvinced. 'He should have just said so then.'

'Crenshaw,' intervened Liz, 'also classifies the poems in the Song as erotic songs, not necessarily related to the marriage ceremony, and that interpretation has gained widespread acceptance in recent years. Did you pick up some of the erotic overtones?'

'The whole thing is riddled with sexual innuendoes,' said Wade with a snigger. 'The woman is like a locked garden, but her lover enters to pick the fruit; he knocks on her door and thrusts his hand (a euphemism in ancient literature for penis) into the "hole" to unlock the door, and her innards "seethe for him", etc., etc. But how much you pick up depends quite a lot on the translation you use. The NRSV, for example, translates 7:2 as "Your navel is a rounded bowl that never lacks mixed wine". Pope's version in his commentary on the Song of Songs is: "Your vulva a rounded crater; May it never lack punch"!'

Melinda looked disgusted, Kirsty blushed, and Maureen said that she couldn't see what a vulva had to do with punch.

Liz explained that the Hebrew word which the NRSV translated 'navel' and Pope 'vulva' is used elsewhere in the Old Testament to refer to the umbilical cord (Ezekiel 16:4) but it is so similar to the Arabic word which means 'secret' or 'pudenda' that some critics think that it may have been used in this instance as a euphemism for vulva. 'Vulva would be appropriate in this context because a "wasf" usually refers to parts of the human body in ascending or descending order. In 7:1–6 the description starts with the woman's feet and works up to her head, and the word in question occurs between a reference to the woman's thighs and her belly. Also, navel's aren't exactly noted for their capacity to produce fluid. Falk,' Liz continued, 'agrees that vulva is probably what is meant, but because English has no word that does not have either clinical or pornographic connotations, she translates the lines "Your hips – a bowl of nectar brimming full".'

'I still think it's rude,' muttered Maureen. 'And it's almost as bad a few lines down when the man compares the woman to a palm tree and her breasts to clusters of dates which he'll climb up and grab.'

'What you need, Maureen, is to be illuminated by the Holy Spirit,' said Frank sternly, 'and then you read the Old Testament in the light of the New. In Ephesians Paul talks about the union between Christ and the Church being like that between husband and wife, and that's the key to understanding the Song of Solomon. When it says "Thy navel is like a round goblet, which wanteth not liquor: thy belly is like an heap of wheat set about with lilies" what it really means is that the bride, the Church, never lacks the wine and bread of the Eucharist, which she receives with a pure faith, symbol- ized by lilies. The palm tree stands for the saints of God: straight, upright, evergreen, unbending, able to withstand storms and desert conditions and bear fruit to a good old age. The righteous shall flourish like a palm tree, praise the Lord! And when the bride says further along in chapter 7 "let us go forth into the field", what she is really saying is "let us go forth into the world to love and serve God". The "pleasant fruits" which she finds at her gate are the fruit of the Holy Spirit, as it says in Galatians 5:22: "love, joy, peace, long suffering, gentleness, goodness, faith, meekness, temperance" ... '

Wade looked at Frank with something akin to wonder.

'I've never been able to understand how people could possibly believe those ludicrous allegorical interpretations of what is patently erotic poetry,' he said. 'Take off your blinkers and you will find that 7:11–14 is a charming little poem in which the woman playfully invites the man to go off to the countryside to see if the vines are sprouting, the blossoms have opened, the pomegranates are flowering, and the mandrakes are giving forth scent. As Falk says, it is a classic spring love poem: "all of nature is mating – why not we too?" Elsewhere in the Song, vines are clearly associated with erotic experiences; the pomegranate was a fertility symbol in ancient culture; and the mandrake plant was used as an aphrodisiac! But, just in case the man misses those not very subtle allusions, the woman frankly says "There will I give you my love". To see in this speech an allegory of the relationship between the Church and Christ, or (if you are a Jew) Israel and Yahweh, is absurd.'

'Yet until recently allegorical interpretations prevailed in

Judaism and Christianity,' pointed out Liz.

'Origen has a lot to answer for,' said Christobel crossly. 'He raved on in the third century that only those who had conquered passion and lust should be able to read the Song lest (shock, horror) it foster carnal desire.'

'Well, he certainly made sure he didn't succumb to carnal desire,' remarked Wade with a grin.

'How?' asked Kirsty naïvely.

'He castrated himself,' replied Wade.

'Which reveals an absolutely appalling view of sexuality,' cried Christobel. 'And it's utterly tragic that scholars who read the Song literally were condemned by the Church, while others like Bernard of Clairvaux in the Middle Ages could drivel on forever about the Song being about the Word and the soul.'

'It's amazing that Bernard could write 86 sermons on just the first two chapters of the Song,' said Ruth. 'I find some of what he says very profound and moving, but he just seems to use verses of the Song as a springboard from which he jumps off into mystical theology.'

'Martin Luther and John Wesley also interpreted the Song allegorically,' revealed Liz, 'and a Congregationalist scholar in the last century maintained that it could not be understood literally because the female speeches were totally contrary to the true nature and modesty of women!'

'I suppose that he couldn't cope with women taking the initiative in love-making and revelling in the joys of sex,' seethed Christobel. 'Of all the ignorant, sexist, male ... '

'I fully accept that the Song of Songs is, on one level at least, a celebration of human love,' interjected Melinda, 'and I have no problems with a celebration of pure, faithful love within the marriage relationship being in sacred Scripture. It was, after all, God who ordained that men and women should marry, and he created us in such a way that when we marry we can experience joy in physical expressions of love … '

'But there is no indication that the couple in the Song are married!' objected Wade.

'Of course there is. The man calls the woman "my spouse" in 4:9–10 and 5:1,' declared Frank.

'Yes, but only in the prudish King James version,' retorted Wade. 'In the NRSV it is "my sister, my bride". Does that mean that their relationship was incestuous?'

'Probably "my sister" and "my bride" are just terms of affection,' said Liz quickly. 'Certainly there is nothing in the Song to indicate that the woman was a wife, with the kind of wifely responsibilities extolled in Proverbs 31: working day and night to feed and clothe her family.'

'They wouldn't be sneaking off to make love in a field, or wishing they could pretend to be brother and sister so that they could kiss in public, if they weren't having a secret affair,' said Maureen reasonably. 'And that reminds me of something else that struck me when I was reading chapter 8. The woman goes on about how she wishes she could bring her lover into her mother's house and feed him pomegranate juice. Actually, there are quite a few references to her mother but none to her father. She must have come from a broken home. But, in any case, when my ex-husband and I were courting I would never have dreamed of taking him to my parent's house to make love. He had an old Mini Minor and we used to go for a drive out of town and park somewhere quiet. Jolly uncomfortable it was, too. And one awful night it rained quite a lot and we got bogged down in mud. We had to walk two miles back to town to get Don's Uncle Fred to pull us out with his old truck. I was never so embarrassed in all my life.'

'I think that parents should treat their grown-up children as adults and let them bring their friends home,' observed Christobel.

'But they must maintain moral standards!' said Melinda looking shocked.

'Yes, well, I accepted the inevitable when my girls grew up,' went on Maureen. 'Never knew how many were going to turn up for breakfast, so I just kept the pantry cupboard stocked with cornflakes and let them help themselves. The funny thing was, it was all right for my son to chase girls, but he got quite upset about other guys getting too close to his sisters. By the sounds of things the woman in the Song of Songs had the same problem with her brothers.'

'It's because of generations of cultural conditioning,' proclaimed Christobel with a toss of her head. 'The ideal man is a super-stud, while the ideal woman is chaste and virtuous. He is always the pursuer, she the pursued. What I love about the Song of Songs is that it completely overturns those tired old stereotypes. The woman is the most prominent of the speakers, and she's just as able to express desire and yearning as the man.'

Liz agreed, and went on to say that translations which refer to the woman as the 'beloved' and the man as the 'lover' really annoy her because the words are identical in Hebrew: whichever lover speaks, he or she refers to the other as the 'beloved'. It's not as though the woman passively receives love: quite the reverse!

'I was absolutely thrilled to read in Phyllis Trible's *God and the Rhetoric of Sexuality* how the Song of Songs redeems "the love story gone awry" in Genesis 2–3,' Christobel went on excitedly. 'I'd never thought about it before, but there are an amazing number of parallels between Genesis 2–3 and the Song. In Genesis the man and woman first experience sexual union in the garden, and it is usually in garden settings that the man and woman in the Song make love. Animals and plants abound in both stories, but in the Song there is no nasty serpent, no ridiculous restrictions on what the lovers can eat, and no tragic act of disobedience. And instead of the break-up of the family foreshadowed in Genesis 2:24 ("therefore a man leaves his father and his mother and clings to his wife"), the woman in the Song actually wants to bring her lover into her mother's house (as you noted, Maureen). However, the most fabulous thing of all is that the consequences of disobedience in Genesis 3 are completely reversed in the Song. Just think of those appalling words in Genesis 3:16 when the woman is told: "in pain you shall bring forth children, yet your desire shall be for your husband, and he shall rule over you". In the Song, on the other hand, the woman is able to say on two occasions: "My beloved is mine and I am his." Isn't that wonderful! There is complete harmony and mutuality – neither partner in the relationship is dominant or subordinate. And in 7:10 the woman can rejoice that "I am my beloved's, and *his desire is for me*" which is exactly the opposite of Genesis 3:16!'

Liz nodded, and pointed out that the Hebrew word for 'desire' is only used in the Old Testament in these two verses. In both cases it clearly refers to sexual desire, but Song of Songs 7:11 not only has the man instead of the woman experiencing the desire, it also completely lacks the negative connotations of Genesis 3:16.

'So,' Liz finished up, glancing at her watch, 'can we conclude, as Pope does in his commentary, that 8:6 ("Love is strong as Death") is "the climax and immortal message of the Sublime Song"?'

'Absolutely, because "Love is strong as Death" is also a wonderful reversal of Genesis 3,' insisted Christobel, jumping up and down in her chair. 'As Trible says, in Genesis 3 "death became the disintegration of life. Harmony gave way to hostility; unity and fulfilment to fragmentation and dispersion". However, in Song of Songs 8:6–7 we have the wonderful assurance (conveyed by the woman, incidentally) that love is the equal of death, and "many waters cannot quench love, neither can floods drown it".'

'She obviously never had kids and a mortgage,' muttered Maureen.

'Romans 8:35–39,' said Frank with a zealous gleam in his eyes, '"Who shall separate us from the love of Christ? Shall tribulation, or distress, or persecution, or famine … "'

'One final question,' Liz put in quickly, 'or two, really: do you agree that Song of Songs belongs in the canon of Scripture, and if so why?'

'I think that it's absolutely wonderful to have an affirmation of the joys of sexual love in the Bible,' replied Christobel firmly. 'Christians have traditionally been so prudish about sex, but why can't we rejoice in the gifts of a loving creator? And Song of Songs provides us with a wonderful vision of what a loving relationship between a man and a woman can and should be like, one based on equality and mutuality. Surely this also says something about Mother-Sophia who created sexuality, and concluded that all her creation was "very good". Actually, the more I think about it, the more convinced I become that Song of Songs must have been written by a woman, and Spirit-Sophia must have worked overtime to get it accepted by patriarchal Jewish and Christian leaders. I know they came up with their silly allegorical interpretations to justify it being in the canon, but at least that way it was preserved for us.'

'I was reading Murphy's commentary on the Song of Songs last night, and he believes that the Song is certainly about human love,' acknowledged Ruth, 'but he also suggests that perhaps the human love so vividly portrayed in the Song could reflect something of God's love. He recommends that we avoid the exaggerations and misunderstandings of past generations of interpreters, but still be open to the possibility that they may have caught a glimpse of the Song's theological significance. I kind of like that approach.'

'Well, I was impressed by E. H. Petersen's arguments in *Five Smooth Stones for Pastoral Work*,' said Melinda. 'I particularly liked the way he related the Song of Songs to the concepts of salvation and covenant. As Liz said earlier, within Judaism the Song of Songs is traditionally read at the time of Passover, which is, of course, the ritual meal which celebrates Israel's great experience of salvation and relationship with God. The Song explores the experience of God's saving love not on the grand scale of the Exodus, but in the intimacies of daily life, and it is in daily life that we too need to encounter God.'

'Has it occurred to you that the Song could be considered "wisdom literature"?' asked Liz.

'The fact that it has traditionally been attributed to Solomon suggests that it is,' responded Wade, 'as Solomon is supposed to be to wisdom literature what Moses is to the law, and David to the psalms. Moreover, wisdom literature is basically human reflection on human existence, and love and sex are obviously a fairly significant part of human existence! But as Childs says in his *Introduction to the Old Testament as Scripture*, probably the clearest indication that the Song is wisdom literature is in 8:6–7 where the woman's speech moves beyond dialogue with her lover or anyone else to a reflective generalization about the nature of love. She then concludes with the aphorism (which could have been plucked straight out of the Book of Proverbs) that you cannot buy love.'

'Yes, we are saved by faith alone,' said Frank.

'So that is why I agree with Pope that 8:6–7 is the climax of the Song,' Wade went on, ignoring Frank. 'The remaining verses are a bit like a post-coital cigarette.'

'My ex-husband always liked to smoke after sex too,' said Maureen. 'Dirty, filthy habit. I'd just as soon have a cup of tea, and talking about tea, isn't it time that we stopped for a break?'

'It certainly is,' said Liz with a laugh. 'But before you go I do want to encourage you to ponder over the literal meaning of the Song before you go rushing off to hunt for so-called "higher" or "spiritual" meanings. Although, having said that, I do find Trible's more allegorical approach insightful. Note, however, that Trible takes the literal meaning of the text seriously before she goes looking for deeper meanings.'

Frank wasn't very impressed, but Kirsty and I agreed on the way out that we had learned quite a lot. Kirsty then excitedly confided that she was going to meet her aunty – who, when she heard about Tweetie Pie's demise, promised to buy her two love-birds!

'I was only going to get one new bird, but you can't really have a single love-bird, can you?'

I agreed that it seemed more appropriate to have two.

'And I might even end up with baby birds!' she exclaimed.

I said that that was something to look forward to.

WEEK·ELEVEN

Prophets

Jason was back today, but still coughing. Dave, reported Liz, was out of hospital, but didn't feel quite up to joining us.

To get the discussion going, Liz asked, 'If you were told that someone is a prophet, what would your immediate reaction be?'

'Wow! He can see into the future!' replied Kirsty at once.

'He's a nutcase,' croaked Jason.

'He's filled with the Holy Spirit,' declared Frank.

'*She* has the most marvellous mystical experiences of God,' cried Christobel. 'Remember that, according to the prophet Joel, God promised that "I will pour out my spirit on *all* flesh; your sons *and your daughters* shall prophesy ... Even on the male *and female* slaves in those days, I will pour out my spirit ... " Isn't that thrillingly non-sexist and non-classist?'

'Of course, Joel's prophecy was fulfilled in the early Church, as it says in Acts,' remarked Melinda. 'We don't have such experiences now. We don't need them. We have the Bible instead. However, I do believe that people who preach the need to repent of sin and believe in the Lord Jesus Christ are following in the footsteps of the biblical prophets.'

'Joel said that God would give the gift of the Spirit in "the last days" and it's still the last days,' argued Frank. 'There are prophets in my Prayer, Praise, and Holy Power fellowship who prophesy every week.'

'I once went to a charismatic church and a man prophesied about me,' confided Kirsty.

'What did he say?' asked Maureen.

'That I was like a rosebud that would gradually unfurl, and I'd be an excellent wife and mother, and God had the right husband planned for me and I'd meet him soon.'

'Humph,' snorted Maureen. 'I don't call that much of a prophecy. You mark my words, before you know where you are you'll be full-blown, with your leaves covered with black spot, and Mr Right will have waltzed off with a glamorous orchid. You'd be much better off concentrating on getting a good career and not worrying about getting married.'

Christobel agreed.

'The Old Testament prophets weren't dating agencies,' exploded Wade. 'They also weren't primarily into predicting what would happen in the future, or preaching the need for repentance, or having mystical experiences of God. They were the *social conscience* of their nation, exposing injustice and oppression, and spelling out its consequences.'

'There are differences of opinion among scholars as to what exactly was the role of ancient Israelite prophets,' intervened Liz. 'They are still a very mysterious phenomenon, but perhaps we can get a clue from the fact that the English word "prophet" is derived from the Greek *prophetes* which seems to mean "one who speaks for another", usually a deity. "Prophets" is often used to translate the Hebrew *nabi* which may mean "one who is called" or "one who calls or proclaims". Consequently, Gene Tucker, in his article in *Prophecy in Israel* (edited by David Peterson), defines an Israelite prophet as someone who experienced a call or summons to speak on behalf of God, and when he spoke it was more often than not to proclaim judgement or salvation. Sorry, Christobel, I said "he", but nearly all the prophets that we know about were men. Miriam and Deborah were, however, called prophets, so it was not an exclusively male vocation. Does anyone disagree with that definition?'

'I like the stress on the fact that the prophets were especially called by God,' asserted Melinda. 'How privileged they were to see into heaven and be personally commissioned to speak on God's behalf, as it says in Isaiah 6, Jeremiah 1, and the beginning of Ezekiel.'

'Those "call narratives" follow a stereotyped pattern,' said Wade dismissively. 'The prophet is confronted by God and commissioned to speak on his behalf. The prophet objects that he can't, is reassured, and then given a sign to confirm God's support. Such narratives were clearly intended to legitimate the prophets' claims to be God's messengers. I'd like more emphasis on the fact that prophets like Amos, Hosea, and Isaiah did not just *proclaim* judgement, they *explained* why it was going to happen, which is much more significant. If you were living in the northern or southern Israelite kingdoms in the eighth century, like they were, you didn't need a crystal ball to tell you that the international political situation was becoming ominous, and Israel and Judah didn't have a hope in hell of withstanding a concerted attack by the Assyrian empire. What really got up the prophets' noses was the arrogance and complacency of the well-to-do people who were living in luxury while they trampled the poor into the dust.'

'But the Israelites' greatest sin was to fall into idolatry,' stated Melinda. 'I find it almost incomprehensible that a people who had been so blessed by God could adopt disgusting, immoral, cultic practices, such as temple prostitutes, orgies ...'

'Sounds like jolly good fun!' exclaimed Jason.

Melinda cast him a withering glance.

'But it wasn't just the prostitutes and their customers who got a ticking-off from God via the prophets,' snapped Wade, 'the supposedly pious Jews were in trouble as well: "I hate, I despise your festivals, and I take no delight in your solemn assemblies …"'

'You both have a point,' intervened Liz firmly. 'Amos and Hosea addressed the northern kingdom of Israel – Amos in the middle of the eighth century and Hosea a little later. Amos certainly attacked gross social injustice, while Hosea focused a bit more on idolatry. Both prophets agreed that the downfall of the kingdom was imminent.'

'And I can't bear those horrid oracles of doom,' said Christobel with a shudder. 'Hosea 13 is absolutely appalling. The prophet must have made a mistake. God could not possibly have wanted little children to be dashed in pieces, or pregnant women ripped open.'

Kirsty grimaced.

'Yes, it does sound horrific,' acknowledged Melinda in an unperturbed way, 'but you must remember, Christobel, that as well as being a God of love, God is a holy God who cannot abide sin. He gave the Israelites plenty of opportunities to repent, which they wilfully ignored, so he had to punish them.'

'But God didn't personally sit up in heaven, directing the Assyrians to dash children against rocks and cut open pregnant women,' burst out Wade. 'Assyria's conquest of Israel in 721 took place with all the horrors associated with war because of Assyria's superior military might. I don't believe that God initiated it any more than he initiated Hitler's conquests in the late 1930s and early 40s. History simply took its course. However, Amos and Hosea took the

169

opportunity to rebuke the Israelites for their sins which had greatly reduced the capacity of the nation to defend itself.'

'And, from a faith perspective, they believed that Yahweh was ultimately in control not just of Israel and Judah but all nations,' said Ruth, 'so he would have to allow the invasion to take place. It was easy to see it as punishment for the people's sins. However, the wonderful thing is, they also believed that if the Israelites repented and turned back to Yahweh, Yahweh would act to restore his chosen people after the devastation.'

'Hosea certainly thought that way,' admitted Liz. 'There is some doubt about Amos. Most scholars believe that the final verses of the last chapter, which contain the promise of restoration, were a later addition, which would make Amos the most negative of all the prophets.'

'Surely, Liz, we do not need to be so sceptical?' said Melinda. 'Amos 9:11–15 is in accordance with the underlying theme running through the Old Testament that the Messiah will come. Verse 11 obviously refers to Jesus Christ.'

'Where is it?' said Wade, flicking through his Bible. 'Ah, yes, just as I thought, there's no mention of the Messiah at all, which, in any case, simply means "the anointed one" and could refer to an earthly king. The "booth of David" that verse 11 says is in ruins and is to be raised up, repaired, and rebuilt is doubtless either the temple or Jerusalem as a whole, not the Davidic dynasty to which Jesus supposedly belonged. And that is clearly a clue that this part of Amos was written after the destruction of Jerusalem in 587 BCE.'

Liz nodded.

'Well, I am sure that even you cannot deny, Wade, that Isaiah prophesied about Christ,' maintained Melinda, glaring at him, '"for a child has been born for us", "he was despised and rejected", etc., etc.'

'The child referred to in Isaiah 9 could have been

Hezekiah, King Ahaz's son, and the description of him as a "mighty warrior", "prince of peace", "wonderful counsellor", etc., simply reflects an idealized view of kingship,' responded Wade coolly. 'Likewise, the suffering servant of the latter part of Isaiah is meant to be the people of God as a whole, not Jesus Christ.'

'As I have said before, I feel sorry for anyone who has so little faith,' proclaimed Melinda. 'I personally find it wonderful that through Isaiah, who lived in Judah in the eighth century BC, God revealed much about his plans for humanity. And it was not just Isaiah's prophecies about the Messiah which were fulfilled – those predicting Judah's fall to Babylon, and her exile and eventual restoration, were clearly vindicated 200 years later.'

'The vast majority of scholars believe that Isaiah didn't write about the Babylonian exile in the eighth century,' retorted Wade. 'Only Isaiah 1–39 can be dated back to his time. Chapters 40–55 (Second Isaiah) were written during the exile, and 56–66 (Third Isaiah) some time after the exiles returned to Judah.'

'I know that some people chose to believe that,' replied Melinda in a lofty tone, 'but I am convinced by the other side of the argument: that the unified structure, and the common language and themes running through the book indicate that it can only have been written by one person.'

'The Bible says that Isaiah was written by Isaiah, and that's good enough for me,' said Frank.

'The general consensus among scholars that parts of Isaiah were written at different times doesn't mean that there are three separate lots of prophecy, one tacked on to the other,' Liz tried to explain. 'Second and Third Isaiah were meant to supplement, help explain, or bring "up to date" First Isaiah, and the whole book was heavily edited so that there is an

171

impression of unity. Older and newer traditions were interwo-
ven, so, for example, parts of 1–39 are probably much later
than the eighth century.'

'But if Isaiah was partly written or edited during the
Babylonian exile, or later in the sixth century, why did who
ever finished it off claim that it was all by the prophet Isaiah?'
asked Kirsty, looking troubled. 'Wasn't that sort of dishonest?'

'You might have read that the Israelite prophets are sometimes divided into the "writing" and "non-writing" prophets,'
said Liz. 'The "non-writing" ones are figures like Nathan,
Elijah, and Elisha who appear in the Deuteronomic history,
while the "writing" ones are those who had books named after
them, like Amos, Hosea, and Isaiah. However, the fact that a
prophet had a book named after him doesn't necessarily mean
that he actually wrote it. Prophets primarily *spoke* on behalf
of God. The prophetic writings that have survived in the Old
Testament are *collections* of prophetic sayings, which were
probably compiled and edited by other people, probably
initially by the prophet's disciples. We know that this
happened from references in Isaiah 8:6 and Jeremiah 36.
And, as time went on, the prophecies were brought "up to
date" and adapted to new situations, as I just said. Those of
Amos and Hosea, for instance, which were originally directed
toward the northern kingdom were edited to make them
apply to the southern kingdom as well.'

'Oh,' said Kirsty, but she didn't look all that reassured.

'I suppose that it really wasn't so important who actually
spoke or wrote down the prophecies, or when this happened,
so long as God's messages got through,' observed Ruth. 'I was
reading Childs' *Introduction to the Old Testament as Scripture*
last night, and if I remember correctly, he says that Second
and Third Isaiah were attributed to the eighth century
for theological reasons. That way they have a broader

significance: they don't just deal with the Israelites' return from exile in the sixth century but with God's redemptive plan for all history. The prophets' words of judgement for sin and forgiveness for repentance transcend their original historical context and apply to people of all generations.'

'Wouldn't it have been fantastic being a prophet back then?' Frank remarked, somewhat wistfully.

'Actually, I think that it would have been pretty terrible,' retorted Maureen. 'It wasn't a very comfortable life, to say the least! Their poor children got called funny names, like "Not Pitied" and "Not My People", they had to go around naked, and they got mocked and spat on and beaten up and imprisoned and chucked down wells. I wouldn't have liked it at all.'

'Neither would I,' agreed Ruth with a laugh. 'But, as a matter of fact, one of the things which I love about the prophets' stories is that their reactions to their many misfortunes were usually so *human*. They might have been especially chosen by God, and had real experiences of divine power and might, but they still got depressed and afraid. Jeremiah at one stage cursed the day on which he was born, and Elijah was so frightened of Queen Jezebel that he fled into the desert, and didn't stop running for days and days. It is some comfort to know that I am not the only one who succumbs to fear and depression at times!'

'In contrast to certain "enthusiasts" today who yearn to be prophets, the genuine Old Testament prophets didn't want to be prophets,' said Wade with a wry smile. 'The classic example is the story of Jonah. When told by God to go to the Assyrian capital, Nineveh, he couldn't set off in the opposite direction quickly enough.'

'Alas, how often we try to flee from God's will!' said Melinda sorrowfully.

'Was Jonah really swallowed by a whale?' asked Kirsty.

'Of course not. It's just a story,' replied Wade. 'And, incidentally, the sea creature wasn't called a whale but a "big fish".'

'Kirsty, the Book of Jonah appears in the Bible as a straightforward historical, biographical narrative,' interjected Melinda, 'and I see no reason to question its veracity. 2 Kings 14:25 contains a brief reference to the prophet Jonah who lived in Israel during the reign of King Jeroboam in the early eighth century, and the author of the Book of Jonah has traditionally been thought to have been this man. He therefore lived at a time when Assyria was becoming an increasing threat to Israel ... '

'Rubbish,' said Wade scornfully. 'Modern scholars conclude that Jonah was written after the exile.'

'If I may be allowed to continue,' said Melinda in an icy tone, 'the main reason, Kirsty, why some people reject the historicity of Jonah seems to be that they cannot believe in the fish miracle. But the Bible is full of miracles! No doubt they also doubt that Jesus rose again! If you believe the Bible you will have no trouble accepting that God could miraculously intervene to change Jonah's course.'

'And there have been cases of people who have really survived being swallowed by fish,' added Frank eagerly. 'My pastor said once ... '

'And pigs can fly and a cow jumped over the moon,' mocked Jason, and then succumbed to a coughing fit.

'But,' continued Melinda loudly, ignoring the interruptions, 'the most important thing to remember, Kirsty, is that our Lord Jesus Christ chose to compare his Resurrection to the story of Jonah. I don't think that he would have done that if the story was just fiction, do you?'

'To start with, Jesus of Nazareth may have wrongly assumed that Jonah was historical,' Wade struck back.

'However, as he often spoke in parables, he probably would have appreciated the story of Jonah regardless of whether it fitted your narrow definition of "truth" or not. It is, above all, a reflection on prophecy which highlights some general "truths" about the role of the prophet. Jonah initially doesn't want to obey God's call, but he has to reluctantly carry out God's will and proclaim God's sentence of judgement on Nineveh. He then gets thoroughly hacked off when God changes his mind and doesn't destroy the city after all.'

'There was a real moral in that for the Israelites,' commented Ruth. 'Even their worst enemies could repent, and God was so merciful that they would be forgiven!'

'Yes,' said Melinda firmly. 'And it clearly shows that we are called to go on missions to other nations … '

'Here we go …' muttered Wade.

'Look, can we just spend a few minutes discussing the role of Israelite prophets in society?' intervened Liz quickly.

'There were two basic roles,' answered Wade before anyone else could speak. 'Within the establishment they legitimated the status quo and whipped up patriotic enthusiasm for wars and suchlike. There is a classic example of that in 1 Kings 22 when the kings of Israel and Judah want to go to war and they ask 400 prophets whether they should go or not, and the prophets assure them that they will be victorious. However, there were also prophets who operated on the periphery of society and challenged the political and religious establishment. In 1 Kings 22 this group is represented by just one man, Micaiah, who prophesies disaster. As a result he gets slapped on the face and put in prison, but it is his prophecy that is vindicated.'

'Well, we know that there are false prophets around,' said Frank. 'John warns us about them in 1 John 4 … '

'But the Hebrew Bible never actually calls the establishment prophets "false prophets",' Wade pointed out. 'In 1 Kings 22 Micaiah accepts that his opponents are prophets, they just happened to be wrong in that particular case. They either deliberately lied, or they really believed that they prophesied authentically. A devout Israelite could well have assumed that Yahweh would protect and support Israel and Judah – that it was inconceivable that the Israelites would be defeated by their evil enemies. Exactly the same kind of sentiments were around in the United States during the Cold War: the Soviet Union stood for all the evils of atheistic communism, while the United States represented Christianity and democracy. God would naturally be on the American side! Church leaders could therefore exhort young men to go off to Vietnam, confident of victory, and confident that they were doing what was right and in accordance with God's will. However, if you ask me, the *true* prophets, the prophets who most authentically spoke on behalf of God, were those who condemned the arms race and opposed the Vietnam War, and tried to expose all the poverty, oppression, racism, and sexism which existed in "the greatest nation on earth". And many of them were mocked, abused, beaten up, arrested and imprisoned, but that's the usual fate of prophets. Some, like Martin Luther King, paid the ultimate price.'

Ruth nodded. 'When I think of prophets today, I think of the conservationists who are trying to make people realize that if we continue to exploit and abuse the earth the outcome will be disastrous,' she added.

'Yes, yes,' cried Wade passionately, leaning forward in his seat and thumping the table with his fist. 'And you don't need a crystal ball to see that disaster is imminent, there are scientific studies aplenty to verify it, but most people are so damned complacent ... just like the eighth-century Israelites!'

'And there are also feminist prophets,' said Christobel, 'who expose patriarchy for the oppressive sinful system that it is. And that's not unrelated to ecological issues, either, because, let's face it, most of the problems in the world have been caused by men, so now we have to get women in positions of responsibility to fix things up.'

'So what do you think of the biblical prophets from a feminist perspective, Christobel?' asked Liz with a smile.

'To start with, it's utterly obvious that they lived in a patriarchal culture,' Christobel responded, waving her hands around. 'They go on and on about Abraham, Moses, etc., and scarcely mention women, and they nearly always speak of God as if she were male. Even more insidious, on the rare occasions when women are mentioned, they are symbols of the Israelites' promiscuity and faithlessness, chasing after foreign gods – while men symbolize the one true God! That's most obvious in Hosea when Hosea gets to play the role of God, and his poor wife Gomer the "adulteress Israel". But at least she gets accepted back in the end. Ezekiel's poor wife symbolizes Judah and has to die, and Ezekiel is commanded not to mourn for her. That's bad enough, but to add insult to injury he doesn't even give her name, she's just another of the many nameless women of the Bible. And Ezekiel carries on with a lot of rubbish about the conduct of Judah before the exile being like the "uncleanness" of a woman with her period, and only male animals could be used as sacrifices at the temple, and all that kind of stuff which makes my blood absolutely boil. But, I must admit, that occasionally, very occasionally, the prophets do portray God in female terms. Second Isaiah has God gasping and panting like a woman in childbirth, and remarking "Can a woman forget her nursing child, or show no compassion for the child of her womb?" Then Third

Isaiah picks the image up and says in 66:13 "As a mother comforts her child, so I will comfort you".'

'And feminist scholars are retrieving those sort of images, and using them to combat the view that God is male,' said Liz. 'Actually, that reminds me of another characteristic of the Israelite prophets. They didn't just look *forward* to what would happen in the future, they looked *back* at the tradition. There was a lot of debate earlier this century about which came first: the prophets or the law. Some argued that as the Pentateuch was put together quite late, it was actually the prophets who deserve most of the credit for the development of Israelite religion. However, there is greater agreement now that a good proportion of the traditions which eventually became part of the Pentateuch predated the prophets, and they would have been familiar with them, as they were with each other's prophecies. They didn't just parrot them, though. They interpreted the traditions and prophecies they received, applied them to their own times, and added their own insights, which often challenged the prevailing ideology. For example, think of how enormously important the temple and animal sacrifices were in Israelite worship, and then read verses like Hosea 6:6: "For I desire steadfast love and not sacrifice, the knowledge of God rather than burnt offerings".'

'And prophets who can say things like that are still needed today,' thundered Wade. 'Ideally, the Church as a whole should have a prophetic role, challenging the political and economic establishments, but so often prophets are needed to expose the Church's own failings.'

'Mmm,' said Maureen. 'Personally I don't want to be the one to stand up and make a fuss, but I usually end up doing it and getting into trouble as a result. The other day I couldn't help saying at my ladies' fellowship meeting that I am fed up with all the committees and rosters and trading tables at our church. Everyone's so busy, busy, busy that no one has any time to visit people who are sick or having problems or just want a bit of friendship. I know for a fact that no one ever comes near my house unless it's to ask me to do something. "Where are our priorities?" I said. "I've worn myself out working for this church over the years, and has it brought me any closer to God? No it has not." Then I remembered that I'd read somewhere once that if the Holy Spirit left the church, eighty or ninety per cent of the work would still go on, so I told them that too. I didn't mean to hurt anyone, but there was dead silence after I stopped speaking and it was pretty clear that some people were real offended.'

'I think that it was very brave of you to speak up,' said Christobel encouragingly.

Maureen shrugged her shoulders. 'At least they'll hopefully stop asking me to do things.'

'To finish up, could we consider for a few minutes how we can use the prophetic writings today?' asked Liz. 'Do they still function as revelation?'

'They are still very valuable,' replied Melinda, 'especially because of their prophecies about the Messiah which, as we know, were fulfilled in Jesus Christ.'

'The New Testament writers started off that sort of interpretation – plucking whatever bits they liked out of the prophetic writings and applying them to Jesus to back up their claims that he was the Messiah,' scoffed Wade. 'It didn't matter that they took them totally out of context.'

'The same Holy Spirit who inspired the prophets inspired the New Testament writers,' maintained Melinda, 'so he could give them insight into the deeper meaning of the prophecies. Likewise, under the inspiration of the Spirit the words could have been reused even if the contexts were different.'

'On one hand, the more that I discover about the historical context in which the prophetic books were written, the more remote they seem,' said Ruth thoughtfully. 'I can see how they were related to the situation at the time, and how they were influenced by the culture of the day. On the other hand, however, it amazes me that so many of the prophets' concerns are still our concerns.'

'There is still poverty, injustice, and oppression,' put in Wade grimly.

'And people still turn away from God and true worship,' added Melinda.

'And people still experience fear and sorrow and doubt and complacency,' contributed Christobel.

'Poor old God,' remarked Maureen sympathetically. 'Two and a half thousand years on, and we're still messing things up.'

'Yes, we certainly still need to hear God's offer of forgiveness and renewal, love and support,' continued Ruth with a rueful smile. '"Do not fear, for I have redeemed you; I have called you by name, you are mine ... " as it says in Isaiah 43:1. You know, another reason why I think that the prophetic literature is so enduring is that much of it is poetry and poetry speaks to the human heart, transcending time and place. For me, anyway, it provides a channel through which God can sometimes reach me. I try to ponder prayerfully over verses like Isaiah 43:1 and Micah 6:8 (" ... what does the Lord require of you but to do justice, and to love kindness, and to walk humbly with your God?") and they still seem so full of meaning.'

'Yes, that's a good note to finish on,' said Liz with a sigh of relief.

As I walked out of the room with Kirsty, I asked how her new love-birds were going.

She looked disconcerted.

'I think they hate each other! First they kept on opposite sides of the cage, then Juliet started pulling Romeo's feathers out. I don't know what to do. How can you teach justice, kindness and mercy to a love-bird?'

I commiserated with her, but couldn't give any advice other than to pray about it. God at least would probably share her frustration!

WEEK·TWELVE

Daniel

Kirsty arrived, puffing and panting, with a small birdcage which she put down on the table with a sigh of relief. 'I almost missed the bus, and then I had to stand all the way,' she gasped. 'But we finally made it.'

'We' turned out to be she and Romeo. She lifted the cover off the cage so that we could see him. Minus most of his feathers, he wasn't a pleasant sight. He was also alone. Kirsty said that she had found Juliet lying lifeless at the bottom of the cage a few mornings ago.

'Are you sure that she was dead?' asked Wade with a faint smile.

Kirsty produced from her bag a shoe box and took the lid off. We all peered in. Nothing could disguise the fact that Juliet was definitely an ex-love-bird.

'Forgive me for asking,' said Liz in a strained voice, 'I know it's a stupid question, but why, Kirsty, have you brought along a live and a dead bird to a Scripture tutorial?'

Kirsty hastily apologized and explained that she had been talking to Dave on the phone last night, and she had told him about Juliet's sudden demise, and Romeo looking so sick, and how she thought she should take him to a vet, but she didn't have a car …

'So Dave said,' continued Kirsty with glowing eyes, 'that if

I brought Romeo along today, he would take us to Otto's vet after the tutorial finished! Wasn't that kind of him?'

'Very,' said Liz through clenched teeth.

'And he also said that he thought that I should bring Juliet's body – in case the vet wants to do a post-mortem, so I dug the poor little thing up.'

That accounted for Juliet's rather dirty appearance.

'Well, I think you should certainly get Romeo to a vet. I must admit, he's the ugliest bird I've ever seen,' said Maureen frankly. 'Even Juliet looks better.'

Romeo screeched something unprintable at her and Kirsty hurriedly put his cover back on. At that moment Dave walked in, with Otto bounding at his side. Otto seemed extremely pleased to join us again. He barked ecstatically, and leaped up at each of us in turn, almost knocking Liz over, scattering Maureen's notes, and (to her horror) licking Melinda's face.

'I'm taking him to the V–E–T for a check-up,' whispered Dave, 'but he doesn't know it yet. Is this Romeo, Kirsty?' Dave removed Romeo's cover and looked shocked at what he saw.

'Good grief! The poor little chap!'

Romeo uttered a rather disgruntled squawk. Otto stopped hunting in Kirsty's bag for any food, raised his head and stood transfixed, staring at Romeo. Romeo stared back at him. We stared at them both.

'I trust that you have recovered from your injuries, Dave?' asked Melinda, breaking the silence at last.

Dave replied that he was on the mend, but he hadn't felt up to doing any reading, and would we please not make him laugh because it hurt too much. Kirsty gazed at him admiringly and said that he was being very brave. Dave gave a self-deprecating smile and said that he wasn't really, but he was obviously pleased when Kirsty hotly disagreed with

Maureen's comment that anyone who played soccer needed their head examined and deserved all the pain they got.

Liz cut short Kirsty's spirited defence of Dave's sporting prowess and begged us to turn our attention to the Book of Daniel.

'I'm afraid that I really have to ask who wrote Daniel and when?'

'Daniel, of course,' replied Frank. 'He was a Jew who was taken captive when King Nebuchadnezzar of Babylon defeated Judah in 605 BC. He lived in Babylon from then until at least three years after its conquest by King Cyrus of Persia in 539. God inspired him to prophesy about the fate of the Babylonian, Medo-Persian, Greek and Roman Empires, who followed one after the other; the coming of the Antichrist, and the savage persecution that will break out in the last days before the Second Coming and the Final Judgement ... '

There was no mistaking the passionate enthusiasm in Frank's voice.

'No serious scholars believe that any more,' groaned Wade. 'On the contrary, Daniel was written between 168 and 164 BCE, 400 years after its supposed historical setting. The author demonstrates only a vague knowledge of the Babylonian and Persian eras in comparison with his much more accurate knowledge of the fate of Alexander the Great's empire, which was divided after his death in 323 BCE by his generals. The Ptolemaic dynasty ruled Egypt and the Seleucid dynasty ruled Syria. Palestine, caught in the middle, suffered from their rivalry and interminable wars. By the second century BCE it was the Seleucids turn to dominate, and between 168/4 the Seleucid king Antiochus IV took harsh measures against Jews. According to Jewish sources he tried to suppress Jewish religion and enforce acceptance of Greek religious and cultural practices.'

'Yes, it must have been a terrible time,' said Ruth. 'In 2 Maccabees 6 it says:

> Harsh and utterly grievous was the onslaught of evil. For the temple was filled with debauchery and revelling by the Gentiles, who dallied with prostitutes and had intercourse with women within the sacred precincts, and besides brought in things for sacrifice that were unfit. The altar was covered with abominable offerings that were forbidden by the laws. People could neither keep the Sabbath, nor observe the festivals of their ancestors, nor so much as confess themselves to be Jews.

'Many people were tortured and killed, just for circumcising their sons or refusing to break the Jewish dietary laws by eating pork ... '

'And you believe that Daniel was written in response to this situation?' asked Liz.

'It seems plausible,' replied Ruth.

'But the Bible says that Daniel was the author,' declared Frank, crossing his arms belligerently.

'It only says that he received visions and put them in writing, it doesn't claim that he wrote the whole book,' said Wade in an exasperated tone. 'And only the visions are written as first person accounts, the stories of his adventures at the royal court are in the third person.'

'It is not impossible that later disciples of Daniel added the third person narratives to the visions,' conceded Melinda, 'but the traditional view has always been that Daniel was the author, and that he wrote in the sixth century. The main reason why liberal scholars refuse to accept this seems to be that they do not believe in miracles or that future events can be accurately predicted ahead of time. As I said last week, miracles and prophecy pose no problems for anyone who believes the Bible, who knows that nothing is impossible to God.'

'Yeah, and Jesus believed that Daniel was the author,' continued Frank triumphantly. 'It says so somewhere in Matthew, and Ezekiel mentions Daniel in Ezekiel 14:14, and he lived during the Babylonian exile so he would have known him for sure.'

'He mentions *a* Daniel as an archetypal wise and righteous man along with Noah and Job,' retorted Wade, 'which is hardly how he would have described a younger contemporary. But, Melinda, it is not just scepticism regarding clearly fantastic miracle stories and prophecies which has led to scholars rejecting a sixth-century date for Daniel. The book is riddled with historical errors! The most notable is that Darius the Mede is supposed to have conquered the Babylonian kingdom (Daniel 5:31). In reality, it was Cyrus the Persian. Darius the Mede never existed!'

'Darius could have been one of Cyrus's generals who was appointed governor of Babylon, a sort of vassal king,' said Melinda, 'or Darius could be another name for Cyrus himself. There must be some explanation.'

Wade gave a derisive snort.

'Don't forget that liberal scholars once thought that the king whom Darius overthrew, King Belshazzar, could not have existed either,' warned Melinda, 'because the name of the king at the time was Nabonidus. However, subsequent research has shown that Belshazzar was Nabonidus's son, and he was regent in Babylon during his father's absence ...'

'Liberal and conservative scholars remain seriously divided over the authorship and date of Daniel,' interjected Liz, 'so I don't think there's much point continuing this discussion. It will just result in a stalemate. Let's turn to a literary approach to the text instead. What sort of literature is it?'

'History and prophecy,' declared Frank.

'Court novelettes and apocalyptic,' countered Wade.

Ignoring Frank, Liz asked Wade to elaborate.

'The first six chapters contain six stories about a character called Daniel at a foreign court,' responded Wade, 'which are clearly fictional to anyone with half a brain. The remainder of the book consists of apocalyptic visions. Most apocalyptic writings date from 200 BCE to 100 BCE, a time when there was a revival of Jewish nationalism, conflict between Jews and Gentiles, divisions within Judaism (not least about what the proper response should be to Gentiles and Gentile cultures), and political, social, and economic crises. Apocalyptic literature was written by oppressed Jews, loyal to traditional values and practices, who were trying to understand why they were suffering.'

'I couldn't make head or tail of all those visions,' confessed Maureen, 'but I read a bit about apocalyptic literature. Let's see, where did I jot it down? … Oh, yes, here we are. Apocalyptic. Comes from the Greek word for "to reveal" or "to uncover". Common characteristics:

- Secret divine revelation made known to special people, often in the forms of dreams, visions, and conversations with angels (like Daniel had), which is different from God speaking directly to the prophets, who had to proclaim his message to all the people.
- Often pseudonymous (what a mouthful that is!). In other words, an apocalypse is presented as revelation given to some famous figure in Israel's dim, distant past which was sealed up and kept hidden until the appointed time for it to be revealed. I suppose that is why Dan is told in 12:4 that he is to keep his visions secret and seal up his book until the end time.

- Highly symbolic and cryptic language. That's what I found really bizarre about it. All those beasts in Daniel with wings and lots of horns and iron teeth and goodness knows what else.
- Spiritual forces, angels and demons … '

'Clearly, authors of apocalyptic literature were influenced by Babylonian and Persian astrology, angelology, demonology, mythology, and so on,' observed Wade, interrupting Maureen.

'But the apocalyptic writers also drew on Jewish wisdom and prophetic writings from the past,' Ruth pointed out, 'and their overall message was in keeping with mainstream Jewish faith: an assurance that God is ultimately in control. There is evil in the world, but God will eventually overrule it. God will win in the end. The godly who suffer and perish for their faith will be raised up to everlasting life, while their enemies will be condemned. That must have been comforting to those enduring persecution in the time of Antiochus IV.'

'Yes, unlike the prophets, who were mostly concerned with the immediate future, the apocalyptic writers' perspective was long-term,' continued Wade. 'History is divided into periods, predetermined by God, and at the end God will bring history to a violent close, defeating evil and delivering the righteous.'

'Praise the Lord!' exclaimed Frank. 'It is going to happen soon. My pastor explained to me that the fourth beast in Daniel represents the revived Roman Empire in the form of the European Union … '

'Well, while on the subject of last things,' intervened Liz, 'this is the last tutorial of this course. Do you have any final reflections about how the course has gone, what you have gained from it?'

'It just seems that everything I learned at Sunday School isn't true!' wailed Kirsty.

'Stories like Noah and the ark, Jonah and the whale, and Daniel in the lions' den might not be historically accurate,' said Ruth in a concerned voice, 'but that does not mean that they are not theologically meaningful. To take Daniel as an example, it seems to me that the first part of Daniel consists of stories which were designed to teach Israelites how to live under foreign rule. Daniel was a hardworking royal official, who took part in the life of the court so long as he did not have to compromise his religious beliefs. When he had to make a choice between obeying God and obeying the king, he obeyed God and bravely faced the consequences. God miraculously delivered him, thus demonstrating that God's power is superior to that of earthly monarchs, God is ultimately in control. Does it really matter whether Daniel was a real person or not?'

'Of course it matters,' exclaimed Melinda, shocked.

'If he's not, then the Bible's a fraud,' declared Frank.

'It just seems to me that much of the Old Testament is made up of either narratives or poetry,' Ruth earnestly tried to explain, 'which convey truth without being necessarily historically accurate. It is not as though the Book of Daniel is presented as Daniel's diary or autobiography. Rather, it contains carefully and artistically constructed *stories* which have settings, plots, characters, themes, a narrator, and so on.'

'And that is why they have been so easy to teach to children,' added Christobel. 'It's just unfortunate that the impression has nearly always been given that they are history, not fiction, and they have not been balanced with stories about women remaining faithful to God. However, there are additions to the Book of Daniel which are in the Apocrypha, and one of them is about Susanna, a beautiful married woman who was absolutely devoted and faithful to God. Two horrible old Jewish elders lusted after her and one day found her alone in her garden. They demanded that she let them have sex with her or else they would raise a hue and cry and say that they had found a young man with her! Poor Susanna refused to give in to them "and sin in the sight of the Lord", so they did what they had threatened, and on their testimony she was condemned to death for adultery. She cried out to God, and God heard her cry and arranged for Daniel to cross-examine the elders and prove that they were lying. That, of course, reveals the underlying patriarchal nature of the story: no one listens to Susanna and she can't speak in her defence. It takes a man to deliver her and then he gets all the credit!'

'But the story of Susanna does show that women as well as men can stand firm in their faith, and God hears the cry of the innocent,' remarked Ruth, 'so surely it can still be inspiring today, regardless of whether Susanna was a real person or not?'

'Well, Kirsty,' said Dave, bending down to pat Otto, who was still trying to out-stare Romeo, 'as far as I am concerned, Daniel was as real a person as you and I are!'

Kirsty looked comforted.

'You just need to have faith,' Frank advised her. 'The trouble with liberal scholars is that they don't have faith. They doubt everything, but I'm *certain* Daniel is true.'

'I once heard someone say,' mused Christobel, 'that the opposite to faith is not doubt, but *certainty*, and I think that is incredibly profound! Think about it!'

'Man's finite mind can never comprehend the infinite mysteries of God,' responded Melinda. 'Faith accepts that there are mysteries which we cannot understand. However, there are some things that we do need to be certain about. We need to know that the Bible *is* God's Word, that it is trustworthy, that it gives us error-free, authoritative revelation about what we must do to be saved ... '

'Yes, well, I still don't understand how God could have inspired the Bible,' complained Maureen. 'Actually, the more I study it, the less likely it seems that he did.'

'That's the trouble with liberal scholarship,' said Melinda angrily, 'once you start doubting one thing, you begin doubting others. It is like a hole in a knitted jumper. If you don't darn it quickly, it keeps getting bigger and bigger.'

'Has anyone any suggestions about how the Bible can be considered revelation, then?' asked Liz. 'What about you, Ruth, are you any further along the road to answering this question than you were at the beginning of the course?'

'It's something that I have been pondering,' Ruth answered slowly, 'and the conclusion that I have come to is that the Bible is the human record of many different peoples' searches for God, experiences of God, and responses to God. I think that the ancient Israelites did have genuine religious experiences, and these were often passed on to others orally, in the form of poems, songs, prayers, prophetic oracles, stories, and so on. Sometimes they were adapted to apply to different circumstances: for example, prophecies originally directed at the northern Israelite kingdom were later applied to the southern kingdom. In time, however, the oral traditions were written down, and eventually the faith community chose which writings most authentically expressed its faith to be included in the canon of Scripture to pass on to future generations.'

'What do you mean by faith community?' asked Maureen.

'The formation of the canon was a long process, I think. Originally, different groups would have cherished certain writings (temple priests for example), but gradually these came to be accepted by the community as a whole. From what I can make out, the Pentateuch or Torah was probably accepted by the fifth century BCE, the prophetic books slightly later, and the rest, lumped together as "the Writings" between the first centuries BCE and CE. Although that doesn't mean that the Bible as we know it now was in its final form by the end of the first century, because Jews, Roman Catholics, Orthodox and Protestants have adopted slightly different canons. The Roman Catholic canon was defined by the Council of Trent in the sixteenth century.'

'So it's the Church that decides,' said Maureen with a nod.

'Interestingly, in the Jewish canon, Daniel belongs amongst "the Writings" and not the prophets,' reflected Liz. 'But, getting back to the point, suppose we assume that the Old Testament contains records of ancient Israelites' experiences of God. We also have to acknowledge that those records consciously and unconsciously reflect the world in which they were written, so what can we conclude about their relevance for us, living several thousand years later?'

'As I said last week, I am constantly amazed at the number of issues addressed by the Old Testament writers which are still of concern to us,' said Ruth, 'and I do believe that when we read Scripture, or hear it proclaimed in church, God can speak to us through it.'

'Yes,' said Liz. 'My understanding of Scripture has been helped by Roger Haight's book, *Dynamics of Theology*. He talks of revelation being *behind* Scripture (the original experiences of God), *embedded* in Scripture (because Scripture is the expression of the original revelation), and *in front* of Scripture (because Scripture can mediate new religious experiences). This flows from his basic conviction that revelation is not information *about* God but an encounter *with* God.'

192

'But the Bible does give us information about God,' pointed out Maureen, 'which raises another problem for me, because actually I don't think that God always comes across as very nice. He loses his temper, changes his mind …'

'Loves and grieves and interacts with humans,' finished Ruth exuberantly. 'Isn't that a welcome contrast to the impassive, impersonal, unchanging, remote supreme being in Greek philosophy? God is passionately interested in creation and involved in all aspects of human life.'

'You have to realize, Maureen,' said Melinda, 'that God is both a holy God who punishes sin and a merciful God who reaches out to save human beings. The Old Testament is the story of God's saving deeds, which, we know, culminate in the New Testament with the sending of his son, Jesus Christ to die for our sins on the Cross …'

'It is the story of a God who acts on behalf of the oppressed,' declared Wade, 'and is close to the poor and needy …'

'But only the parts which aren't oppressive or demeaning to women can be considered divine revelation,' interjected Christobel. 'We need to get rid of all the horrid patriarchal stuff. For instance, that vision in Daniel of God as an old man with a beard has been frightfully influential in shaping people's ideas of God, and of course it is totally inaccurate, like all those loopy interpretations of when the Second Coming will occur and who will be the Antichrist. If you ask me, the author of Daniel must have had a bad attack of indigestion, and people have been silly enough to take his nightmares literally.'

'The Bible warns us that in the last days people will turn away from the truth and false teachers will arise,' began Frank heatedly, but he was interrupted by Jason walking into the room. Otto burst into ferocious barking before realizing that

Jason was to be greeted as a friend not an intruder. Eventually he calmed down and returned to staring at Romeo.

'What a day I've had!' moaned Jason, throwing his sports bag on the floor and collapsing into a chair. 'I went away for the weekend and when I got home Deidre had disappeared. I'd left her loose in the bathroom, swinging from the shower rail, but the water was cut off for some time and she managed to escape down the loo. I thought I'd lost her for good, but she turned up in the next street. I saw her on the news last night. Some old couple were having a fit because they'd discovered a snake in their lounge. Poor Deidre was freezing after being stuck in the sewerage pipes, and just looking for a place to warm up. Anyway, she ended up at the zoo, and I've just spent hours getting her back.'

'She's not with you now, is she?' exclaimed Kirsty, looking at Jason's bag with wide eyes and shrinking closer to Dave.

'No, she was so traumatized by being gawked at by a bus load of pre-schoolers at the zoo that she got under the car seat and wouldn't come out. I've parked the car in the sun so it should keep warm enough for her.'

'Now that you are here, do you have any final reflections on the course, Jason?' asked Liz.

Jason scratched his head.

'I suppose that I didn't know much about the Old Testament when we started, and what I did know seemed pretty weird, but now I feel as though I've got a greater appreciation of the historical background of the writings, and they make more sense. I've also got a better understanding of the Bible as literature, and how there's lots of stories and poetry and stuff that you don't have to interpret literally. But I guess that what has struck me most is that everyone has their own little "Bible reading spectacles" which they put on whenever they read it, and what they read is obviously coloured by their own particular tinted glass.'

'Yes, there is no neutral way to approach the Bible,' agreed Liz.

'But there must be objective truth in the Bible, otherwise it's just "anything goes",' cried Melinda.

'Oh, I don't think "anything goes", replied Ruth. 'Biblical scholars have their work judged by their academic peers, and if they come up with theories which are too fanciful or implausible their work will not have much credibility and their reputations will suffer. Likewise, hierarchies of the different churches and the faith communities they represent can also decide which interpretations most accurately reflect their experiences of God ... '

'What we need is communities of women to read and interpret the Bible,' proclaimed Christobel. 'Rich and poor, black and white, married and single, lesbian and hetero-sexual ... '

Frank nearly choked at the prospect.

'Michael, you haven't said much this semester,' said Liz. 'How have you found the course?'

I confessed that I had been pretty confused to start off with, and I wasn't sure that I was very much the wiser now. Perhaps fully understanding the mosaic of ancient holy writ-ings that we call the Old Testament is a lifetime's task – not one that can be accomplished in twelve weeks!

For once everyone agreed.

Suggested Further Reading

An enormous number of books have been written about the Bible. The following is just a brief selection of those which I have found helpful.

General Reading

Anderson, B. W. *The Living World of the Old Testament*. 4th edition. Harlow, Essex: Longman, 1988.

Barr, J. *Escaping from Fundamentalism*. London: SCM Press, 1984.

Biggs, C. R. & Catlin, A. L. G. *A Way into the Old Testament*. Revised edition. Melbourne: Uniting Church Press, 1988.

Brown, R. E., Fitzmeyer, J. A. & Murphy, R.E., eds. *The New Jerome Biblical Commentary*. Englewood Cliffs, New Jersey: Prentice Hall, 1990.

Charpentier, E. *How to Read the Old Testament*. London: SCM Press, 1982.

Childs, B. S. *Introduction to the Old Testament as Scripture*. Philadelphia: Fortress Press, 1979.

Crenshaw, J. L. *Old Testament, Story and Faith: A Literary and Theological Introduction*. Peabody, Massachusetts: Hendrickson Publishers, 1986.

Dillard, R. B. & Longman, T., III. *An Introduction to the Old*

Testament. Grand Rapids, Michigan: Zondervan, 1994.

Efird, J. M. *How to Interpret the Bible*. Atlanta: John Knox Press, 1984.

Fee, G. D. & Stuart, D. *How to Read the Bible For All Its Worth: A Guide to Understanding the Bible*. 2nd edition. Grand Rapids, Michigan: Zondervan, 1993.

Fiorenza, E. Schussler. *Bread Not Stone: The Challenge of Feminist Biblical Interpretation*. Edinburgh: T. & T. Clark, 1990.

Gottwald, N. K. *The Hebrew Bible. A Socio-Literary Introduction*. Philadelphia: Fortress Press, 1985.

Hayes, J. H. & Holladay, C. R. *Biblical Exegesis: A Beginner's Handbook*. Revised edition. Atlanta: John Knox Press, 1987.

Laffey, A. L. *An Introduction to the Old Testament: A Feminist Perspective*. Philadelphia: Fortress Press, 1988.

Newsom, C. A. & Ringe, S. H., eds. *The Women's Bible Commentary*. Louisville, Kentucky: Westminster/John Knox Press, 1992.

Ord, D. R. & Coote, R. B. *Is the Bible True? Understanding the Bible Today*. London: SCM, 1994.

Parker, K. I. *Text and Tradition: A Guide to the Old Testament*. Burlington, Ontario: Trinity Press, 1990.

Rogerson, J. W., ed. *Beginning Old Testament Study*. London: SPCK, 1983.

Ryken, L. & Longman, T., III. *A Complete Literary Guide to the Bible*. Grand Rapids, Michigan: Zondervan, 1993.

Spong, J. S. *Rescuing the Bible from Fundamentalism: A Bishop Rethinks the Meaning of Scripture*. San Francisco: HarperSanFrancisco, 1991.

Tate, W. R. *Biblical Interpretation: An Intergrated Approach*. Peabody, Massachusetts: Hendrickson Publishers, 1991.

Trible, P. *God and the Rhetoric of Sexuality*. Overtures to

Biblical Theology. Philadelphia: Fortress Press, 1978.

And in Particular ...

WEEKS ONE AND TWO

Hayes, J. H. & Holladay, C. R. *Biblical Exegesis: A Beginner's Handbook*. Revised edition. Atlanta: John Knox Press, 1987.

Ord, D. R. & Coote, R. B. *Is the Bible True? Understanding the Bible Today*. London: SCM, 1994.

Clines, D. J. A. "Method in Old Testament Study" in J. W. Rogerson, ed. *Beginning Old Testament Study*. London: SPCK, 1983.

WEEKS THREE AND FOUR *Genesis*

Brueggeman, W. *Genesis, Interpretation: A Biblical Commentary for Teaching and Preaching*. Atlanta: John Knox Press, 1982.

Rogerson, J. *Genesis 1–11*. Journal for the Society of Old Testament Study, 1991.

Westermann, C. *Genesis: A Practical Commentary*. Translated by D. Green. Grand Rapids, Michigan: Eerdmans, 1987.

WEEK FIVE *Exodus*

Childs, B. S. *Exodus*. Old Testament Library. London: SCM, 1974.

Durham, J. I. *Exodus*. Word Biblical Commentary. Waco, Texas: Word Books, 1987.

Hyatt, J. P. *Exodus*. The New Century Bible Commentary. Revised edition. London: Marshall, Morgan & Scott, 1980.

WEEK SIX *The Deuteronomic History*

Fretheim, T. E. *The Deuteronomic History*. Interpreting Biblical Texts. Nashville: Abingdon Press, 1983.

Nicholson, E. W. *Deuteronomy and Tradition*. Oxford: Basil Blackwell, 1967.

Olson, D. T. *Deuteronomy and the Death of Moses: A Theological Reading*. Overtures to Biblical Theology. Minneapolis: Fortress Press, 1994.

WEEK SEVEN *Job*

Habel, N. C. *The Book of Job: A Commentary*. Old Testament Library. London: SCM Press, 1985.

Perdue, L. G. & Gilpin, W. C., eds. *The Voice from the Whirlwind: Interpreting the Book of Job*. Nashville: Abingdon Press, 1992.

Zuck, R. B., ed. *Sitting With Job: Selected Studies on the Book of Job*. Grand Rapids, Michigan: Baker Book House, 1992.

WEEK EIGHT *Psalms*

Brueggemann, W. *The Message of the Psalms. A Theological Commentary*. Augsburg Old Testament Studies. Minneapolis: Augsburg, 1984.

Holladay, W. L. *The Psalms Through Three Thousand Years. Prayerbook of a Cloud of Witnesses*. Minneapolis: Fortress Press, 1993.

Westermann, C. *The Living Psalms*. Edinburgh: T & T Clark, 1989.

WEEK NINE *Proverbs and Ecclesiastes*

Collins, J. J. *Proverbs, Ecclesiastes*. Knox Preaching Guides. Atlanta: John Knox Press, 1980.

Crenshaw, J. L. *Old Testament Wisdom: An Introduction*. London: SCM, 1981.

Perdue, L. G., Scott, B. B. & Wiseman, W. J., eds. *In Search of Wisdom: Essays in Honour of John G. Gammie*. Louisville, Kentucky: Westminster/John Knox Press, 1993.

WEEK TEN *Song of Songs*

Falk, M. *Love Lyrics from the Bible: A Translation and Literary Study of the Song of Songs*. Sheffield: The Almond Press, 1982.

Pope, M. H. *Song of Songs*. New York: Doubleday, 1965.

Snaith, J. G. *Song of Songs*. The New Century Bible Commentary. London: Marshall Pickering, 1993.

WEEK ELEVEN *Prophets*

Petersen, D. L., ed. *Prophecy in Israel*. Issues in Religion and Theology 10. London: SPCK, 1987.

Sawyer, J. F. A. *Prophecy and the Prophets of the Old Testament*. The Oxford Bible Series. Oxford: Oxford University Press, 1987.

Wilson, R. R. *Prophecy & Society in Ancient Israel*. Philadelphia: Fortress Press, 1980.

WEEK TWELVE *Daniel*

Collins, J. J. *Daniel, 1–2 Maccabees*. Old Testament Message. Wilmington, Delaware: Michael Glazier, 1981.

Goldingay, J. E. *Daniel*. Word Biblical Commentary. Dallas, Texas: Word Books, 1989.

Towner, W. S. *Daniel, Interpretation: A Bible Commentary for Teaching and Preaching*. Atlanta: John Knox Press, 1984.